Accounting for Veterinary Practices

Steven M. Bragg

AccountingTools®

ISBN 978-1-64221-150-4

For more information about AccountingTools® products, visit our Web site at www.accountingtools.com.

Table of Contents

Accounting for Veterinary Practices 1

Introduction 1

The Chart of Accounts 1

The Balance Sheet 5

The Income Statement 6

The Purpose of Financial Statements 8

Best Practices for Financial Reporting 8

Cash Basis vs. Accrual Basis Accounting 10

Recording Transactions in an Accounting System 11
    Double Entry Accounting 11
    The Accruals Concept 12
    Journal Entries 13

Billing and Collection Activities 16

Sales Tax Remittances 16

Calculating and Recording Bad Debts 17
    Direct Write-Off Method 18
    Allowance for Doubtful Accounts 18

Procurement Card Processing 19
    The Procurement Card Reconciliation 19

Processing Expense Reports 20
    The Review of Expense Reports 21

Accounting for Fixed Assets 22
    Fixed Asset Classifications 22
    Initial Measurement of a Fixed Asset 23
    Depreciation Concepts 23
    The Straight-Line Method 24
    MACRS Depreciation 25
    Accounting for Leasehold Improvements 27
    Depreciation Accounting Entries 27
    Accumulated Depreciation 28
    Asset Disposal Accounting 29

Accounting for the Cost of Goods Sold 31

Accounting for Payroll Transactions 31
    Primary Payroll Journal Entry 32
    Accrued Wages 33
    Accrued Bonuses 34
    Manual Paycheck Entry 35
    Employee Advances 36

Accrued Vacation Pay 37
Tax Deposits 39

Closing the Books...*39*
The Accruals Concept 39
Adjusting Entries..40
Reversing Entries..40
Common Adjusting Entries 42
Update Reserves 44
Reconcile the Bank Statement..44
Calculate Depreciation 47
Record All Payables 47
Reconcile Accounts...48
Review Financial Statements..50
Accrue Tax Liabilities 50
Close the Month 50

Veterinary Practice Financial Analysis..*51*

Relevant Accounting Controls *51*

Fraud Indicators..*56*

Cost Control *56*

Summary..*57*

Glossary...**58**

Index **60**

About the Author

Steven Bragg, CPA, has been the chief financial officer or controller of four companies, as well as a consulting manager at Ernst & Young. He received a master's degree in finance from Bentley College, an MBA from Babson College, and a Bachelor's degree in Economics from the University of Maine. He has been a two-time president of the Colorado Mountain Club, and is an avid alpine skier, mountain biker, and certified master diver. Mr. Bragg resides in Centennial, Colorado. He has written more than 300 books and courses, including *New Controller Guidebook*, *GAAP Guidebook*, and *Payroll Management*.

Steven maintains the accountingtools.com web site, which contains continuing professional education courses, the Accounting Best Practices podcast, and thousands of articles on accounting subjects.

Buy Additional AccountingTools Courses

AccountingTools offers more than 1,500 hours of CPE courses, with concentrations in accounting, auditing, finance, taxation, and ethics. Related courses that you might like include:

- Accounting for Managers
- Accounting Information Systems
- Accounting Procedures Guidebook
- Bookkeeping Guidebook
- Fixed Asset Accounting
- Payroll Management

Go to accountingtools.com/cpe to view these additional courses.

Accounting for Veterinary Practices

Introduction

The accounting for a veterinary practice can be fairly complicated, because of the number of services provided and profit centers to be operated. To clarify matters, this book is intended to lay out the essential elements for what is needed to successfully operate the accounting system for a veterinary practice.

The Chart of Accounts

A good starting point for an accounting system is the chart of accounts. This is a listing of all accounts used in the general ledger. *Accounts* are the financial records of a business, while the *general ledger* is used to store accounting information, which is then aggregated into the financial statements produced by a veterinary practice.

The chart of accounts is usually sorted in order by account number, to ease the task of locating specific accounts. The account numbers are usually numeric, but can also be alphabetic or alphanumeric. Accounts are usually listed in order of their appearance in the financial statements, starting with the balance sheet and continuing with the income statement. A sample chart of accounts appears in the following exhibit. In this exhibit, we have used three-digit account coding, which is the simplest format. The 100-series codes are assigned to current assets (those that are used within one year), while the 200-series codes are assigned to fixed assets (those used over a more extended period of time). The 300-series codes are assigned to a catchall "other" category. The 400-series codes are assigned to current liabilities (those that will be settled within one year), while the 500-series codes are assigned to ownership accounts.

> **Note:** For an even longer and more detailed chart of accounts, see the website of the American Animal Hospital Association (AAHA)[1]. It may not be necessary to use such a long chart of accounts, if your practice does not engage in all of the activities shown on the AAHA's chart of accounts.

Sample Veterinary Practice Chart of Accounts – Balance Sheet Accounts

Account Code	Account Name	Description
110	Petty cash	The current balance of petty cash
120	Cash – Checking account	The current checking account balance
130	Cash – Money market	The current money market account balance
140	Accounts receivable	The total amount billed to customers, not yet paid
145	Allowance for bad debts	The best estimate of receivables that will not be paid
150	Drugs and medical supplies	The cost of all drugs and medical supplies on hand

[1] https://www.aaha.org/practice-resources/running-your-practice/chart-of-accounts/

Account Code	Account Name	Description
160	Prepaid expenses	The amount of expenses paid for items not yet consumed
210	Buildings	Fixed asset – Cost of buildings owned by the practice
220	Computer equipment	Fixed asset – Cost of computer equipment owned by the practice
230	Land	Fixed asset – Cost of any land owned by the practice
240	Leasehold improvements	Fixed asset – Cost of any improvements made to leased property
250	Medical equipment	Fixed asset – Cost of any medical equipment owned by the practice
260	Office equipment	Fixed asset – Cost of any office equipment owned by the practice
270	Vehicles	Fixed asset – Cost of any vehicles owned by the practice
275	Accumulated depreciation	Fixed asset – The accumulated amount of any depreciation charged against fixed assets to date
300	Other assets	The cost of any other assets not included in the other asset accounts
400	Accounts payable	The unpaid amount of all trade payables to suppliers
410	Line of credit	The unpaid balance on a line of credit with the bank
420	Current portion of long-term loans	The portion of any long-term debt payable within one year
430	Unearned revenue	Any revenues received but not yet earned
440	Accrued liabilities	Any liabilities for which no supplier invoice has yet been received
450	Payroll taxes payable	Any payroll taxes incurred but not yet paid
460	Workers compensation payable	Any workers compensation liability not yet paid
470	Sales and use taxes payable	Any sales or use taxes incurred but not yet paid
480	Income taxes payable	Any income taxes incurred but not yet paid
490	Long term liabilities	Any liabilities payable in more than one year
500	Common stock	The par value amount of any common stock sold
510	Additional paid-in capital	The amount in excess of par value for any common stock sold
520	Retained earnings	The amount of practice earnings not paid out
530	Treasury stock	The cost of any common stock repurchased by the practice

A sample chart of accounts for those accounts that will be rolled up into the income statement appear in the following exhibit. In the exhibit, we continue to use three-digit account coding, where the 600-series codes are assigned to revenue accounts, and the 700-series codes are assigned to expense accounts that can be aligned with revenue accounts. The 800-series accounts are for general and administrative activities that are not directly associated with any revenue-generating activities. Where possible, we have set up expense accounts that correspond to a related revenue account, so that the two can be matched to see if a profit or loss has been generated for each activity.

Sample Veterinary Practice Chart of Accounts – Income Statement Accounts

Account Code	Account Name	Description
600	Exam revenue	Includes routines exams, minor wound care, and services
605	Vaccination revenue	Includes fees for the administration of vaccines
610	Hospitalization revenue	Includes all hospitalization and inpatient services
615	Diagnostic services revenue	Includes all measurements and tests conducted
620	Rehabilitation revenue	Includes fees for all types of rehabilitation activities
625	Mortuary revenue	Includes fees for cremation, cemetery plots, caskets, and so forth
630	Pharmacy revenue	Includes the sale of all prescription medications
635	Dietary product revenue	Includes food sold for therapy and general wellness
640	Laboratory revenue	Includes in-house and outside lab work
645	Imaging revenue	Includes fees for x-rays, CT scans, ultrasound, and so forth
650	Surgery revenue	Includes fees related to surgery activities and related supplies
655	Anesthesia and sedatives revenue	Includes all anesthetic products administered, plus monitoring
660	Ancillary products revenue	Includes over-the-counter products and related
665	Boarding revenue	Includes fees from boarding and daycare services
670	Grooming revenue	Includes fees from bathing and grooming services
675	Miscellaneous revenue	Includes all revenue generated outside of the preceding categories
680	Discounts and returns	Includes offsets to revenues for fee discounts and product returns
700	Exam expenses	Includes the cost of all materials used during animal examinations
705	Vaccination expenses	Includes the cost of animal vaccine products
710	Hospitalization expenses	Includes all direct costs incurred when animals are hospitalized
715	Diagnostic expenses	Includes all direct costs incurred when conducting diagnostics
720	Rehabilitation expenses	Includes all direct costs associated with rehabilitation activities
725	Mortuary expenses	Includes all direct costs related to cremation and burial activities
730	Pharmacy expenses	Includes the cost of all pharmaceutical products sold
735	Dietary product expenses	Includes the cost of all dietary products sold
740	Laboratory expenses	Includes all direct costs related to billed laboratory services
745	Imaging expenses	Includes all direct costs related to billed imaging services
750	Surgery expenses	Includes all direct costs related to billed surgery services
755	Anesthesia and sedatives expenses	Includes all direct costs related to billed anesthesia and sedatives
760	Ancillary products expenses	Includes the cost of all ancillary products sold
765	Boarding expenses	Includes all direct costs related to billed boarding expenses
770	Grooming expenses	Includes all direct costs related to grooming expenses

Account Code	Account Name	Description
800	Compensation expense	Includes all wages and salaries paid by the practice
802	Contractor expenses	Includes all contractor fees paid by the practice
804	Employer payroll tax expense	Includes the employer-paid share of all payroll taxes
806	Employee benefit expense	Includes all employee benefits paid by the practice
808	Insurance expense	Includes all types of non-health care expenses paid by the practice
810	Training expense	Includes all training and continuing education fees
812	Travel and entertainment expense	Includes all travel, housing, and meals incurred on practice business
814	Facility rent expense	Includes the facility rent
816	Equipment rent expense	Includes all rental fees for equipment used by the practice
818	Lease expense	Includes all property leasing fees
820	Service contracts	Includes all ongoing service contracts to which the practice is a party
822	Maintenance and janitorial expense	Includes all facility maintenance and janitorial expenses incurred
824	Real estate taxes	Includes all real estate taxes incurred
826	Vehicle expenses	Includes the cost of vehicles used by the practice
828	Utilities expense	Includes all electricity, phone, water, sewage and other related expenses
830	Trash disposal expense	Includes the cost of the practice's trash disposal
832	Licenses and permits expense	Includes all the ongoing cost of licenses, permits, and dues
834	Office supplies	Includes all office supplies acquired for the practice
836	Postage and printing expense	Includes all postage and printing charges incurred
838	Accounting and legal fees	Includes all accounting and legal fees billed by outside parties
840	Advertising expense	Includes all types of advertising expenses incurred
842	Bank fees	Includes any fees charged by the practice's bank(s)
844	Depreciation expense	Includes the period depreciation on fixed assets
846	Interest expense	Includes all interest incurred on debts of the practice
848	Income tax expense	Includes all federal, state, and local income taxes incurred
850	Miscellaneous expense	Includes all other expenses incurred

Note: We have spread out the account numbers in the preceding chart of accounts, so that additional account codes can be inserted as necessary.

In the preceding income statement chart of accounts exhibit, we make repeated references to the "direct cost" of an activity. A *direct cost* is any cost that is only incurred in relation to an activity. So, if the activity does not occur, then the related direct cost is not incurred. This is a critical issue, for any profit center analysis (as explained later) should only include the direct costs associated with a profit center. *Indirect costs* (those that do not change with a change in activity) should not be included in a profit center analysis.

Tip: It makes more sense to subdivide the compensation expense account into several sub-accounts, since this is the largest expense classification. By tracking this expense at a fine-grained level, you can more easily spot expense anomalies. Conversely, it makes little sense to sub-divide a smaller expense classification, such as bank fees, since it accumulates very little expense.

The Balance Sheet

A veterinary practice should produce a *balance sheet* at the end of each reporting period (which is probably on a monthly basis). This report shows the total assets, liabilities, and owners' equity as of the final day of the reporting period. A sample balance sheet appears in the following exhibit.

Sample Veterinary Practice Balance Sheet

ASSETS	
Current Assets	
Cash	$150,000
Accounts receivable (net)	40,000
Drugs and medical supplies	90,000
Prepaid expenses	20,000
Fixed assets (net)	600,000
Other assets	100,000
TOTAL ASSETS	$1,000,000
LIABILITIES AND EQUITY	
Current Liabilities	
Accounts payable	$80,000
Line of credit	60,000
Current portion of long-term loans	20,000
Unearned revenue	10,000
Other liabilities	70,000
Total Current Liabilities	240,000
Long term liabilities	150,000
Total Liabilities	390,000
Equity	
Common stock	30,000
Retained earnings	580,000
Total Equity	610,000
TOTAL LIABILITIES AND EQUITY	$1,000,000

The balance sheet reports the amount of assets, liabilities, and equity. An *asset* is an expenditure that has utility through multiple future reporting periods. If an expenditure does not have such utility, it is instead considered an expense. For example, a veterinary practice pays its electricity bill. This expenditure covers something (electricity) that only had utility during the billing period, which is a past period; therefore, it is recorded as an expense. Conversely, the practice buys an x-ray machine, which it expects to use for the next ten years. Since this expenditure has utility through multiple future periods, it is recorded as an asset.

A *liability* is a legally binding obligation payable to another entity. Liabilities are incurred in order to fund the ongoing activities of a business. Examples of liabilities are accounts payable, accrued expenses, wages payable, and taxes payable. These obligations are eventually settled through the transfer of cash or other assets to the other party.

Equity is the net amount of funds invested in a business by its owners, plus any earnings that have been retained within the business. It is also calculated as the difference between the total of all recorded assets and liabilities on the practice's balance sheet.

The Income Statement

A veterinary practice needs to produce an *income statement* at the end of each reporting period (which is probably on a monthly basis). This report shows the revenue generated during the reporting period, from which all expenses incurred during that period are subtracted, leaving a profit or loss. An example of an income statement appears in the following exhibit.

Sample Veterinary Practice Income Statement

Gross revenue	$2,350,000
Less: Discounts and returns	-50,000
Net revenue	2,300,000
Cost of goods sold	500,000
Gross margin	1,800,000
General and administrative expenses	1,500,000
Net operating income	300,000
Interest expense	10,000
Income tax expense	70,000
Net income	$220,000

The preceding income statement sample is extremely compressed, with nearly all revenue and expense accounts being aggregated into a few line items, such as gross revenue and general and administrative expenses. You can produce a more detailed income statement through your accounting software by opting for a version that includes most (or all) of the underlying accounts. It all depends on the level of detail that you want to see. An expanded version appears in the next exhibit. An even longer version could be created that includes every revenue and expense account stated in the chart of accounts, though some degree of aggregation is easier to read.

Sample Expanded Veterinary Practice Income Statement

Gross Revenue	
Exam revenue	$275,000
Vaccination revenue	180,000
Hospitalization revenue	1,750,000
Diagnostic revenue	145,000
Discounts and returns	-50,000
Net Revenue	2,300,000
Cost of Goods Sold	
Exam expenses	60,000
Vaccination expenses	40,000
Hospitalization expenses	380,000
Diagnostic expenses	20,000
Gross Margin	1,800,000
General and Administrative Expenses	
Compensation expense	1,100,000
Contractor expenses	100,000
Employer payroll tax expense	70,000
Employee benefit expense	20,000
Insurance expense	10,000
Facility rent expense	77,000
Maintenance and janitorial expense	20,000
Utilities expense	12,000
Office supplies	5,000
Accounting and legal fees	6,000
Depreciation expense	80,000
Net Operating Income	300,000
Interest Expense	10,000
Income Tax Expense	70,000
Net Income	$220,000

The Purpose of Financial Statements

Why do you need financial statements for a veterinary practice? The main reason is so that you can make informed decisions about the operations of the business. For example, a close examination of the income statement will reveal whether specific operations are operating at a loss or breakeven, and so may be in need of a pricing adjustment. Or, a review of the balance sheet may show that the business is not spinning off sufficient cash to pay off the mortgage on the practice's office building, which may call for an adjustment in the mortgage terms (or more drastic measures). It is especially useful to view the financial statements on a trend line over many months, to see if there are any longer-term trends that can be resolved immediately, rather than waiting until later, when the firm is in crisis mode.

Depending on the complexity of the firm's operations, it can be quite useful to segment the income statement into departments, each of which is set up as a profit center. A *profit center* is a department that generates revenues and profits or losses. It is more complicated to report at the profit center level, since revenues and expenses must be assigned to each one, along with the compensation of the people working in these departments. It may also be useful to allocate overhead to each profit center. For example, a veterinary practice might set up profit centers for the diagnostic services, rehabilitation, surgery, and boarding departments. With this information in hand, it is much easier to determine how much profit is being generated by each segment of the business.

Best Practices for Financial Reporting

There are a number of best practices that you can follow when producing financial statements for a veterinary practice. They are as follows:

- *Minimize account changes*. It is easier to track changes in revenues and expenses if you don't add or delete accounts. When you make one of these changes, transactions end up in other accounts, making them more difficult to compare across multiple reporting periods.
- *Use account definitions*. When entering a transaction, which account to record it in may not be so obvious. To clarify matters, create a definitions list that clearly states which types of transactions should be recorded in each account.
- *Produce financials fast*. When possible, allocate enough staff time to produce financial statements immediately after the end of each month. By doing so, you can spot anomalies in your operations that can be fixed at once. If you delay in producing the financials, then your corresponding corrective actions will be similarly delayed.
- *Have a CPA check your system*. Even if you do not pay for an annual audit (a common occurrence), have a certified public accountant review your accounting system once a year, to see if it is operating correctly. The CPA might spot systemic issues, such as weak controls, that increase your risk of producing incorrect financial statements or losing money due to fraud.

- *Set up profit centers.* Create reports for your profit centers, so that you can review revenues and profits for each one, and spot issues early.
- *Develop key performance indicators (KPIs).* Maintain a short list of the measurements that you think are the most critical to your veterinary practice, such as the average client billing, average number of clients seen per month, and bad debt percentage. These measurements should be reported alongside the financial statements, to give you a more comprehensive view of the organization's performance. A list of common KPIs appears in the following exhibit.
- *Conduct a multi-month scan.* Produce an income statement that reports revenues and expenses for every month of the year-to-date. Scan across each line item, looking for spikes and drops in the reported amounts that represent anomalies, and investigate each one.
- *Compare the results to benchmark performance figures.* Compare your results to the industry average, to see how your practice's performance compares to that of other veterinary practices.
- *Adjust for ownership issues.* If the owners are taking unusually high or low compensation, or receiving unusual benefits (such as sports tickets), adjust the income statement to account for them. Otherwise, the reported profit or loss may be unusually high or low when compared to industry averages.

Tip: When conducting a multi-month scan, adopt a policy of only investigating variances over a certain threshold value, such as $250 or 10%. Otherwise, you will spend an inordinate amount of time examining line items that have a certain amount of natural variability over time, which will result in few actionable items.

Common Key Performance Indicators for a Veterinary Practice

- Administrative staff per full-time-equivalent veterinarian
- Client cancellation rate
- Doctor and staff productivity
- Expenses as a percent of total revenue
- Number of new clients
- Overtime hours worked
- Practice average transaction charge
- Revenue by category
- Revenue centers as a percent of total revenue
- Staff productivity
- Staff turnover
- Staff/doctor ratio
- Total active clients
- Total practice revenue
- Total practice transactions
- Wait times

Cash Basis vs. Accrual Basis Accounting

The *accrual basis of accounting* is the concept of recording revenues when earned and expenses as incurred. This concept differs from the *cash basis of accounting*, under which revenues are recorded when cash is received, and expenses are recorded when cash is paid. For example, a veterinary practice operating under the accrual basis of accounting will record a sale as soon as it issues an invoice to a customer, while a cash basis practice would instead wait to be paid before it records the sale. Similarly, an accrual basis practice will record an expense as incurred, while a cash basis practice would instead wait to pay its supplier before recording the expense.

The accrual basis tends to provide more even recognition of revenues and expenses over time than the cash basis, and so is considered the most valid accounting system for ascertaining the results of operations and financial position of a business. In particular, it supports the *matching principle*, under which revenues and all related expenses are to be recorded within the same reporting period; by doing so, it should be possible to see the full extent of the profits and losses associated with specific business transactions within a single reporting period.

EXAMPLE

The All Paws on Deck Clinic conducts an extensive surgery on an Irish Wolfhound in February, for which it invoices the customer $5,000, to be paid in 30 days. The clinic also incurs $200 of anesthesia costs on its debit card, for which payment is immediately extracted from the practice's bank account. Under the accrual basis of accounting, both the revenue and expense would appear in the February income statement, showing the full impact of the job. However, under the cash basis of accounting, only the anesthesia cost would appear as an expense in February, with the customer billing appearing a month or two later, when the customer pays the bill.

The accrual basis requires the use of estimated reserves in certain areas. For example, a veterinary practice should recognize an expense for estimated bad debts that have not yet been incurred. By doing so, all expenses related to a revenue transaction are recorded at the same time as the revenue, which results in an income statement that fully reflects the results of operations. These estimates may not be entirely accurate, and so can lead to materially inaccurate financial statements. Consequently, care must be used when estimating reserves.

The cash basis of accounting requires little accounting knowledge to operate, which makes it a favorite of many veterinary practices. Nonetheless, this approach to recording transactions suffers from the following problems:

- *Accuracy*. The cash basis yields less accurate results than the accrual basis of accounting, since the timing of cash flows does not necessarily reflect the proper timing of changes in the financial condition of a business. Generally, cash basis accounting tends to result in more reported peaks and valleys in financial performance, due to the lumpy nature of revenue and (especially) expense recognition.

- *Manipulation*. A veterinary practice can alter its reported results by not cashing received checks or altering the payment timing for its liabilities.
- *Lending*. Lenders do not feel that the cash basis generates overly accurate financial statements, and so may refuse to lend money to a business reporting under the cash basis.
- *Audited financial statements*. Auditors will not approve financial statements that were compiled under the cash basis, so a veterinary practice will need to convert to the accrual basis if it wants to have audited statements.
- *Management reporting*. Since the results of cash basis financial statements can be inaccurate, management reports should not be issued that are based upon it.

In short, the numerous problems with the cash basis of accounting may cause an organization to use the accrual basis of accounting.

Recording Transactions in an Accounting System

A *transaction* is a business event that has a monetary impact on a practice's financial statements, and is recorded as an entry in its accounting records. Examples of transactions are paying a supplier for goods delivered, paying an employee for hours worked, and receiving payment from a client.

How do you record a transaction in your accounting system? In most cases, the software manufacturer has developed a simple form structure, so you simply click on the transaction type (such as a client billing or a cash receipt) and then fill in the form that has been presented to you. In other cases, a more specialized format is called for, which is a journal entry. Before we delve into journal entries, you will need to understand the concept of double entry accounting.

Double Entry Accounting

Double entry accounting is a record keeping system under which every transaction is recorded in at least two accounts. There is no upper limit on the number of accounts used in a transaction, but the minimum is two accounts. There are two columns in each account, with debit entries on the left and credit entries on the right. In double entry accounting, the total of all debit entries must match the total of all credit entries. When this happens, a transaction is said to be *in balance*. If the totals do not agree, the transaction is *out of balance*. An out of balance transaction must be corrected before financial statements can be created.

The definitions of a debit and credit are:

- A *debit* is an accounting entry that either increases an asset or expense account, or decreases a liability or equity account. It is positioned to the left in an accounting entry.

11

- A *credit* is an accounting entry that either increases a liability or equity account, or decreases an asset or expense account. It is positioned to the right in an accounting entry.

An account is a separate, detailed record associated with a specific asset, liability, equity, revenue, expense, gain, or loss. Examples of accounts are noted in the following table:

Characteristics of Sample Accounts

Account Name	Account Type	Normal Account Balance
Cash	Asset	Debit
Accounts receivable	Asset	Debit
Supplies inventory	Asset	Debit
Fixed assets	Asset	Debit
Accounts payable	Liability	Credit
Loans payable	Liability	Credit
Common stock	Equity	Credit
Retained earnings	Equity	Credit
Revenue	Revenue	Credit
Cost of goods sold	Expense	Debit
Compensation expense	Expense	Debit
Utilities expense	Expense	Debit
Travel and entertainment	Expense	Debit
Gain on sale of asset	Gain	Credit
Loss on sale of asset	Loss	Debit

The key point with double entry accounting is that a single transaction always triggers a recordation in *at least* two accounts, as assets and liabilities gradually flow through a veterinary practice and are converted into revenues, expenses, gains, and losses.

The Accruals Concept

An *accrual* is a journal entry that is used to recognize revenues and expenses that have been earned or consumed, respectively, and for which the related source documents have not yet been received or generated. Accruals are needed to ensure that all revenue and expense elements are recognized within the correct reporting period, irrespective of the timing of related cash flows. Without accruals, the amount of revenue, expense, and profit or loss in a period will not necessarily reflect the actual level of economic activity within a business. Accruals are a key part of the closing process used to create financial statements under the accrual basis of accounting; without accruals, financial statements would be considerably less accurate.

It is most efficient to initially record most accruals as reversing entries. This is a useful feature when a veterinary practice is expecting to issue an invoice to a customer or receive an invoice from a supplier in the following period. For example, a bookkeeper may know that a supplier invoice for $20,000 will arrive a few days after the end of a month, but she wants to close the books as soon as possible. Accordingly, she records a $20,000 reversing entry to recognize the expense in the current month. In the next month, the accrual reverses, creating a negative $20,000 expense that is offset by the arrival and recordation of the supplier invoice.

Examples of accruals that a business might record are:

- *Expense accrual for interest.* A local lender issues a loan to a veterinary practice, and sends the borrower an invoice each month, detailing the amount of interest owed. The borrower can record the interest expense in advance of invoice receipt by recording accrued interest.
- *Expense accrual for wages.* A veterinary practice pays its employees once a month for the hours they have worked through the 26th day of the month. The practice can accrue all additional wages earned from the 27th through the last day of the month, to ensure that the full amount of the wage expense is recognized.

If a veterinary practice records its transactions under the cash basis of accounting, it does not use accruals. Instead, the organization records transactions only when it either pays out or receives cash.

Journal Entries

Journal entries are used in a double entry accounting system, where the intent is to record every business transaction in at least two places. For example, when a practice sells products for cash, this increases both the revenue account and the cash account. Or, if supplies inventory is acquired on account, this increases both the accounts payable account and the inventory account.

The structure of a journal entry is:

- A header line may include a journal entry number and entry date.
- The first column includes the account number and account name into which the entry is recorded. This field is indented if it is for the account being credited.
- The second column contains the debit amount to be entered.
- The third column contains the credit amount to be entered.
- A footer line may also include a brief description of the reason for the entry.

Thus, the basic journal entry format is:

	Debit	Credit
Account name / number	$xx,xxx	
Account name / number		$xx,xxx

The structural rules of a journal entry are that there must be a minimum of two line items in the entry, and that the total amount entered in the debit column equals the total amount entered in the credit column.

A journal entry is usually printed and stored in a binder of accounting transactions, with backup materials attached that justify the entry.

There are several types of journal entries, including the following:

- *Adjusting entry.* An adjusting entry is used at month-end to alter the financial statements to bring them into compliance with the relevant accounting rules and regulations. For example, a veterinary practice could accrue unpaid wages at month-end in order to recognize the wages expense in the current period.
- *Compound entry.* This is a journal entry that includes more than two lines of entries. It is frequently used to record complex transactions, or several transactions at once. For example, the journal entry to record a payroll usually contains many lines, since it involves the recordation of numerous tax liabilities and payroll deductions.
- *Reversing entry.* This is an adjusting entry that is reversed as of the beginning of the following period, usually because an expense was accrued in the preceding period, and is no longer needed. Thus, a wage accrual in the preceding period is reversed in the next period, to be replaced by an actual payroll expenditure.

In general, journal entries are not used to record high-volume transactions, such as client billings or supplier invoices. These transactions are handled through specialized software modules that present a standard on-line form to be filled out. Once the form is complete, the software automatically creates the accounting record.

The following journal entry examples are intended to provide an outline of the general structure of the more common entries encountered. It is impossible to provide a complete set of journal entries that address every variation on every situation, since there are thousands of possible entries.

In each of the following journal entries, we state the topic, the relevant debit and credit, and additional comments as needed.

Revenue journal entries:

- *Sales entry.* Debit accounts receivable and credit sales. If a sale is for cash, the debit is to the cash account instead of the accounts receivable account.

- *Allowance for doubtful accounts entry.* Debit bad debt expense and credit the allowance for doubtful accounts. When actual bad debts are identified, debit the allowance account and credit the accounts receivable account, thereby clearing out the associated invoice.

Expense journal entries:

- *Accounts payable entry.* Debit the asset or expense account to which a purchase relates and credit the accounts payable account. When an account payable is paid, debit accounts payable and credit the cash account.
- *Payroll entry.* Debit the wages expense and payroll tax expense accounts, and credit the cash account. There may be additional credits to account for deductions from benefit expense accounts, if employees have permitted deductions for benefits to be taken from their pay.
- *Accrued expense entry.* Debit the applicable expense and credit the accrued expenses liability account. This entry is usually reversed automatically in the following period.
- *Depreciation entry.* Debit depreciation expense and credit accumulated depreciation. These accounts may be categorized by type of fixed asset.

Asset journal entries:

- *Cash reconciliation entry.* This entry can take many forms, but there is usually a debit to the bank fees account to recognize changes made by the bank, with a credit to the cash account. There may also be a debit to office supplies expense for any check supplies purchased and paid for through the bank account.
- *Prepaid expense adjustment entry.* When recognizing prepaid expenses as expenses, debit the applicable expense account and credit the prepaid expense asset account.
- *Fixed asset addition entry.* Debit the applicable fixed asset account and credit accounts payable.
- *Fixed asset derecognition entry.* Debit accumulated depreciation and credit the applicable fixed asset account. There may also be a gain or loss on the asset derecognition.

Liability journal entries:

See the preceding accounts payable and accrued expense entries.

Equity journal entries:

- *Dividend declaration.* Debit the retained earnings account and credit the dividends payable account. Once dividends are paid, this is a debit to the dividends payable account and a credit to the cash account.
- *Stock sale.* Debit the cash account and credit the common stock account.

These journal entry examples are only intended to provide an overview of the general types and formats of accounting entries. There are many variations on the entries presented here that are used to deal with a broad range of business transactions.

Billing and Collection Activities

When treating a patient, the diagnosis and treatment is checked off on a travel sheet, which is a document that lists every service provided by the practice. The servicing veterinarian documents the services provided during a patient visit, signs the document, and then drops it off at the front desk, where it is entered into the system and payment is obtained. In some practices, an electronic system takes the place of the travel sheet.

In most cases, payment is collected at the time of the patient visit, thereby keeping the practice's accounts receivable to a minimum. A billing to be paid later is usually only allowed when an emergency service results in such a large billing that the client does not have the financial resources to immediately pay the bill. This is a critical issue for a veterinary practice, since the risk of non-collection on receivables is quite high – and also requires an investment in collection staff to obtain payment.

Note: If a client has pet insurance, this usually does not impact the billing and collection process, because the client submits a claim to the insurance company for reimbursement; the practice is not involved.

Since the billing and collection process is essentially being completed at the front desk, it is imperative that a billing and collection specialist be seated at the front desk at all times. If this process is mishandled, then the practice could lose a significant amount of cash from incorrect billings and collections.

Note: Include on a new patient form the requirement that all fees are to be paid at the time of the client's visit – stated in caps. Clients should initial this statement to indicate that they understand the practice's payment terms. The payment terms can also be posted in the waiting area. The intent is to ensure that clients are aware that payment is due when they leave the facility.

Sales Tax Remittances

A veterinary practice is required to charge customers a sales tax on certain types of sales transactions if it is located in the territory of a government entity that charges the sales tax. For example, a practice might have to charge customers the sales tax of the city in which it is located, as well as the county sales tax and the state sales tax.

All accounting software includes a billing feature that allows you to charge sales tax on those items for which it is required (such as sales of pet shampoo). When sales tax is charged, the practice will collect it from clients and then remit it to the state government, which in turn pays it out to the various local governments.

When a business charges a sales tax to a client, the journal entry is a debit to the accounts receivable asset for the entire amount of the invoice, a credit to the sales account for that portion of the invoice attributable to goods or services billed, and a credit to the sales tax liability account for the amount of sales taxes billed.

At the end of each month (or longer, depending on the remittance arrangement with the government), the bookkeeper fills out a sales tax remittance form that itemizes sales and sales taxes, and sends the government the amount of the sales tax recorded in the sales tax liability account.

EXAMPLE

Billabong Veterinary sells a pet treadmill to a client. Billabong issues an invoice for $1,000 of goods delivered, on which there is a seven percent sales tax. The entry is:

	Debit	Credit
Accounts receivable	1,070	
Sales		1,000
Sales taxes payable		70

Following the end of the month, Billabong remits the sales tax withheld to the state government. The entry is:

	Debit	Credit
Sales taxes payable	70	
Cash		70

Later in the following month, the client pays the full amount of the invoice. The entry is:

	Debit	Credit
Cash	1,070	
Accounts receivable		1,070

When a firm bills its clients for sales taxes, those taxes are not an expense to the practice; they are an expense to the clients. From the perspective of the practice, these sales tax billings are liabilities to the local government until remitted.

Calculating and Recording Bad Debts

If the decision is made to offer sales to clients on credit, it is quite likely that some invoices will never be paid. If so, the bookkeeper must write off these invoices as bad debts. There are two ways to do so, which are covered in this section under the headings of the direct write-off method and the allowance for doubtful accounts.

Direct Write-Off Method

The direct write-off method is the practice of charging bad debts to expense in the period when individual invoices have been clearly identified as bad debts. The specific activity needed to write off an account receivable under this method is to create a credit memo for the customer in question, which exactly offsets the amount of the bad debt. Creating the credit memo will require a debit to a bad debt expense account and a credit to the accounts receivable account.

The method does not involve a reduction in the amount of recorded sales, only an increase of the bad debt expense. For example, a veterinary practice records a sale on credit of $1,000 for a surgical procedure, and records it with a debit to the accounts receivable account and a credit to the sales account. After two months, the client is only able to pay $800 of the open balance, so the practice must write off $200. It does so with a $200 credit to the accounts receivable account and an offsetting debit to the bad debt expense account. Thus, the revenue amount remains the same, the remaining receivable is eliminated, and an expense is created in the amount of the bad debt.

The direct write off method delays the recognition of expenses related to a revenue-generating transaction, and so is considered an excessively aggressive accounting method, since it delays some expense recognition, making a veterinary practice appear more profitable in the short term than it really is. For example, it may recognize $50,000 in sales in one period, and then wait three or four months to collect all of the related accounts receivable before finally charging some items off to the bad debt expense. This creates a lengthy delay between revenue recognition and the recognition of expenses that are directly related to that revenue. Thus, the profit in the initial month is overstated, while profit is understated in the month when the bad debts are finally charged to expense.

The direct write off method can be considered a reasonable accounting method if the amount that is written off is an immaterial amount, since doing so has a minimal impact on a firm's reported financial results.

Allowance for Doubtful Accounts

The allowance for doubtful accounts is a reduction of the total amount of accounts receivable appearing on the balance sheet. This allowance represents your best estimate of the amount of accounts receivable that will not be paid in the future by clients.

If the firm is using the accrual basis of accounting, it should record an allowance for doubtful accounts, since this approach provides an estimate of future bad debts that improves the accuracy of the financial statements. Also, by according the allowance at the same time it records a sale, you can properly match the projected bad debt expense against the related sale in the same period, which provides a more accurate view of the true profitability of a sale.

For example, a veterinary practice records $30,000 of sales to a number of clients, and projects (based on historical experience) that it will incur 1% of this amount as bad debts, though it does not know exactly which clients will default. It records the 1% of projected bad debts as a $300 debit to the bad debt expense account and a $300 credit to the allowance for doubtful accounts. The bad debt expense is charged to expense right away, and the allowance for doubtful accounts becomes a reserve account that offsets the account receivable of $30,000 (for a net receivable outstanding of $29,700).

Later, a client defaults on an invoice totaling $200. Accordingly, the practice credits the accounts receivable account by $200 to reduce the amount of outstanding accounts receivable, and debits the allowance for doubtful accounts by $200. This entry reduces the balance in the allowance account to $100. The entry does not impact earnings in the current period.

Procurement Card Processing

A procurement card is the same as a credit card. It is issued to an authorized buyer for the practice, who can buy goods up to a certain dollar limit, and within certain categories of goods and services. The practice then pays the procurement card provider from a single master billing. The use of procurement cards is ideally directed at the 80% of all purchases that comprise 20% of the dollar volume of a business; thus, the cards are designed for low-cost, high-volume purchases.

The advantage of procurement cards lies in their extremely efficient nature from a paperwork perspective. The procurement card provider aggregates all purchases on a single monthly statement, which is subject to a monthly review by the card user, and is then paid. This aggregation process is vastly more efficient than the cumbersome issuance of purchase orders for individual purchases, which should be restricted to only the most expensive acquisitions.

In this section, we describe a reconciliation process for procurement cards.

The Procurement Card Reconciliation

The bank supplying procurement cards to a veterinary practice issues a statement of card activity once a month. The bookkeeper passes this information along to the authorized procurement card user, who is expected to reconcile the statement to his or her purchasing records. The procedure for reconciling a procurement card statement is outlined next:

1. **Match receipts to statement.** Upon receipt of the monthly card statement from the bookkeeper, match all stored receipts to the line items on the statement.
2. **Obtain missing receipts.** If the receipts associated with some line items are missing, contact the supplier to see if a replacement receipt can be obtained. If a receipt cannot be obtained (which is likely), fill out a missing receipts form. This form itemizes any statement line item for which there is no receipt and states the purpose of the expense. The card user signs the form to certify that the expenses on the form are valid business expenses.

> **Tip:** Adopt a cutoff level for the missing receipts form, below which no entries are required. Otherwise, employees may spend an inordinate amount of time documenting insignificant expenditures.

3. **Note disputed charges.** If line item amounts appear to be incorrect or charged in error, circle them on the account statement and note that they are in dispute. Also, complete the disputed expenditure form, which is used by the bookkeeper to follow up with the card provider.
4. **Assign account numbers.** Write the account number to be charged next to each line item on the statement.
5. **Sign approval block.** Before forwarding the card statement, the bookkeeper should have stamped an approval block on it, within which the card user and the practice owner should sign if they approve the expenditures listed in the statement.
6. **Forward documents.** Assemble the card statement, missing receipts form, disputed expenditure form, and receipts into a packet. Make a copy of the packet and retain it. Forward the original version of the packet to the bookkeeper.
7. **Process as normal.** The bookkeeper verifies that all necessary forms are attached to the card reconciliation, and that the document has been approved. The procurement card payment is then handled as a normal account payable.

Processing Expense Reports

The expense report form comes in many varieties, of which there are two main types. The first is shown in the following sample format, where a common set of expense categories are listed across the top row, leaving space for many entries down the left side of the form. The alternative is to switch these placements, so that columns for each of the seven days of the week are listed across the top, with the most common expense categories listed down the left side. The format shown here has the advantage of being usable for longer periods than one week.

Sample Expense Report Form

20

Both expense report formats contain information blocks at the bottom of the report, in which employees can enter additional detailed information about certain expense categories.

The Review of Expense Reports

When a veterinary practice uses a manual submission process for expense reports, there is an enhanced risk of errors in the reports. This procedure gives direction to the reviewers who examine expense reports prior to issuing payments to the submitting employees. The expense report review procedure follows.

1. **Review for non-reimbursement items.** Review the expense report to see if it contains any of the items noted in the following exhibit. If so, they are to be disallowed and subtracted from the expense report. Send an e-mail to the employee, detailing all disallowed expenses, and copy the message to the employee's supervisor.

Sample List of Non-Reimbursement Items

Adult entertainment	Expenses > 90 days old	Personal reading material
Car washes and cleaning	Finance charges on credit cards	Theft/loss of personal property
Contributions	Health club / spa fees	Toiletries
Child care	Laundry fees on short-duration trips	Traffic fines
Clothing	Lost luggage	Travel insurance
Commuting costs	Movies	Undocumented expenses

2. **Match to receipts.** Compare the expenses claimed on the expense report to the accompanying receipts, and request additional information if some receipts are missing.

> **Tip:** It is painfully time-consuming to review every receipt associated with an expense report. An alternative is to examine 100% of the receipts for the largest expenses, and some lesser percentage of the receipts for smaller expenses.

3. **Review per diem meals.** Verify from the travel records in the expense report the dates on which travel was conducted, and verify that per diem charges were only applied for during those dates. Also verify that the per diem rates are correct, and that no actual meal expenditures are included in the expense report in addition to per diem charges.
4. **Review mileage claims.** Review the amount of mileage reimbursement claims for reasonableness. This might include running a mileage calculation on an online travel site. If the miles claimed figure is within a certain percentage of the calculated amount, accept it.

5. **Verify clerical accuracy.** Re-summarize the totals in the expense report for both rows and columns. If the expense report is based on an electronic spreadsheet, it is particularly likely that someone might have added rows or columns that are not reflected in the grand totals on the report.

Accounting for Fixed Assets

The typical veterinary practice owns a significant number of fixed assets, so we provide an expanded treatment of the accounting for fixed assets in this section, including the range of possible classification, depreciation concepts, asset disposals, and the related accounting entries.

Fixed Asset Classifications

If an expenditure qualifies as a fixed asset, it must be recorded within an account classification. Account classifications are used to aggregate fixed assets into groups, so that the same depreciation methods and useful lives can be applied to them.

You also usually create general ledger accounts by classification, and store fixed asset transactions within the classifications to which they belong. Here are the most common classifications used:

- *Buildings*. This account may include the cost of acquiring a building, or the cost of constructing one. If the purchase price of a building includes the cost of land, apportion some of the cost to the Land account (which is not depreciated).
- *Computer equipment*. This classification can include a broad array of computer equipment, such as routers, servers, and backup power generators. It is useful to set the capitalization limit[2] higher than the cost of desktop and laptop computers, so that an excessive number of these assets are not tracked.
- *Equipment*. This category includes all types of medical equipment.
- *Furniture and fixtures*. This is one of the broadest categories of fixed assets, since it can include such diverse assets as office cubicles and desks.
- *Intangible assets*. This is a non-physical asset, examples of which are trademarks, client lists, and patented technology.
- *Land*. This is the only asset that is not depreciated, because it is considered to have an indeterminate useful life. Include in this category all expenditures to prepare the land for its intended purpose, such as demolishing an existing building, or grading the land.
- *Land improvements*. Include any expenditures that add functionality to a parcel of land, such as irrigation systems, fencing, and landscaping.
- *Leasehold improvements*. These are improvements to leased space that are made by the tenant, and typically include office space, air conditioning, telephone wiring, and related permanent fixtures.

---

[2] The capitalization limit is the amount paid for an asset, above which it is recorded as a long-term asset. If the amount paid is less than the capitalization limit, then the amount paid is instead charged to expense in the period incurred.

- *Office equipment.* This account contains such equipment as copiers, printers, and video equipment. Some firms elect to merge this classification into the furniture and fixtures classification, especially if they have few office equipment items.
- *Software.* Includes larger types of practice-wide software, such as a patient scheduling system. Many desktop software packages are not sufficiently expensive to exceed the corporate capitalization limit.
- *Vehicles.* This account contains automobiles, trucks, and similar types of rolling stock.

Initial Measurement of a Fixed Asset

Initially record a fixed asset at the historical cost of acquiring it, which includes the costs to bring it to the condition and location necessary for its intended use. If these preparatory activities will occupy a period of time, also include in the cost of the asset the interest costs related to the cost of the asset during the preparation period.

The activities involved in bringing a fixed asset to the condition and location necessary for its intended purpose include the following:

- Physical construction of the asset
- Demolition of any preexisting structures
- Renovating a preexisting structure to alter it for use by the buyer
- Administrative and technical activities during preconstruction for such activities as designing the asset and obtaining permits
- Administrative and technical work after construction commences for such activities as litigation, labor disputes, and technical problems

Depreciation Concepts

The purpose of *depreciation* is to charge to expense a portion of an asset that relates to the revenue generated by that asset. This is called the matching principle, where revenues and expenses both appear in the income statement in the same reporting period, which gives the best view of how well a firm has performed in a given accounting period. The trouble with this matching concept is that there is usually only a tenuous connection between the generation of revenue and a specific asset.

To get around this linkage problem, we usually assume a steady rate of depreciation over the useful life of each asset, so that we approximate a linkage between the recognition of revenues and expenses. This approximation threatens our credulity even more when a firm uses accelerated depreciation, since the main reason for using it is to defer taxes (and not to better match revenues and expenses).

If we were not to use depreciation at all, we would be forced to charge all assets to expense as soon as we buy them. This would result in large losses in the months when the purchase transaction occurs, followed by unusually high profitability in those periods when the corresponding amount of revenue is recognized, with no offsetting expense. Thus, a veterinary practice that does not use depreciation will have front-loaded expenses, and extremely variable financial results.

There are three factors to consider in the calculation of depreciation, which are as follows:

- *Useful life*. This is the time period over which it is expected that an asset will be productive. Past an asset's useful life, it is no longer cost-effective to continue operating the asset, so a veterinary practice would dispose of it or stop using it. Depreciation is recognized over the useful life of an asset.
- *Salvage value*. When a practice eventually disposes of an asset, it may be able to sell the asset for some reduced amount, which is the salvage value. Depreciation is calculated based on the asset cost, less any estimated salvage value. If salvage value is expected to be quite small, it is generally ignored for the purpose of calculating depreciation.

EXAMPLE

The Waggie Veterinary Clinic buys a company car for $40,000 and estimates that its salvage value will be $10,000 in five years, when it plans to dispose of the car. This means that Waggie will depreciate $30,000 of the asset cost over five years, leaving $10,000 of the cost remaining at the end of that time. Waggie expects to then sell the car for $10,000, which will eliminate it from Waggie's accounting records.

- *Depreciation method*. Depreciation expense can be calculated using an accelerated depreciation method, or evenly over the useful life of the asset. The advantage of using an accelerated method is that you can recognize more depreciation early in the life of a fixed asset, which defers some income tax expense recognition to a later period. The advantage of using a steady depreciation rate is the ease of calculation. An example of an accelerated depreciation method is the MACRS method (as described later). The primary method for steady depreciation is the straight-line method.

The Straight-Line Method

Under the straight-line method, you would depreciate an asset at the same standard rate throughout its useful life. To do so, recognize depreciation expense evenly over the estimated useful life of an asset. The straight-line calculation steps are:

1. Subtract the estimated salvage value of the asset from the amount at which it is recorded on the books.
2. Determine the estimated useful life of the asset. It is easiest to use a standard useful life for each class of assets.
3. Divide the estimated useful life (in years) into 1 to arrive at the straight-line depreciation rate.
4. Multiply the depreciation rate by the asset cost (less salvage value).

EXAMPLE

The Spaniels Forever Clinic purchases a diagnostic machine for $6,000. It has an estimated salvage value of $1,000 and a useful life of five years. The bookkeeper calculates the annual straight-line depreciation for the machine as follows:

1. Purchase cost of $6,000 – Estimated salvage value of $1,000 = Depreciable asset cost of $5,000
2. 1 ÷ 5-Year useful life = 20% Depreciation rate per year
3. 20% Depreciation rate × $5,000 Depreciable asset cost = $1,000 Annual depreciation

MACRS Depreciation

MACRS depreciation is the tax depreciation system used in the United States. MACRS is an acronym for Modified Accelerated Cost Recovery System. Under MACRS, fixed assets are assigned to a specific asset class. The Internal Revenue Service has published a complete set of depreciation tables for each of these classes. The classes are noted in the following table. Those assets that may be found in a veterinary clinic have been stated in bold.

MACRS Table

Class	Depreciation Period	Description
3-year property	3 years	Tractor units for over-the-road use, race horses over 2 years old when placed in service, any other horse over 12 years old when placed in service, qualified rent-to-own property
5-year property	5 years	**Automobiles**, taxis, buses, trucks, **computers and peripheral equipment, office equipment**, any property used in research and experimentation, breeding cattle and dairy cattle, appliances and etc. used in residential rental real estate activity, certain green energy property
7-year property	7 years	**Office furniture and fixtures**, agricultural machinery and equipment, any property not designated as being in another class, natural gas gathering lines
10-year property	10 years	Vessels, barges, tugs, single-purpose agricultural or horticultural structures, trees/vines bearing fruits or nuts, qualified small electric meter and smart electric grid systems
15-year property	15 years	Certain land improvements (such as shrubbery, fences, roads, sidewalks and bridges), retail motor fuel outlets, municipal wastewater treatment plants, clearing and grading land improvements for gas utility property, electric transmission property, natural gas distribution lines
20-year property	20 years	Farm buildings (other than those noted under 10-year property), municipal sewers not categorized as 25-year property, the initial clearing and grading of land for electric utility transmission and distribution plants

Class	Depreciation Period	Description
25-year property	25 years	Property that is an integral part of the water distribution facilities, municipal sewers
Residential rental property	27.5 years	Any building or structure where 80% or more of its gross rental income is from dwelling units
Nonresidential real property	39 years	An office building, store, or warehouse that is not residential property or has a class life of less than 27.5 years

The depreciation rates associated with the more common asset classes are noted in the following exhibit.

Depreciation Rates for MACRS Asset Classes

Recovery Year	3-Year Property	5-Year Property	7-Year Property	10-Year Property	15-Year Property	20-Year Property
1	33.33%	20.00%	14.29%	10.00%	5.00%	3.750%
2	44.45%	32.00%	24.49%	18.00%	9.50%	7.219%
3	14.81%	19.20%	17.49%	14.40%	8.55%	6.677%
4	7.41%	11.52%	12.49%	11.52%	7.70%	6.177%
5		11.52%	8.93%	9.22%	6.93%	5.713%
6		5.76%	8.92%	7.37%	6.23%	5.285%
7			8.93%	6.55%	5.90%	4.888%
8			4.46%	6.55%	5.90%	4.522%
9				6.56%	5.91%	4.462%
10				6.55%	5.90%	4.461%
11				3.28%	5.91%	4.462%
12					5.90%	4.461%
13					5.91%	4.462%
14					5.90%	4.461%
15					5.91%	4.462%
16					2.95%	4.461%
17						4.462%
18						4.461%
19						4.462%
20						4.461%
21						2.231%

Depreciation is calculated for tax reporting purposes by aggregating assets into the various classes noted in the preceding exhibit and using the depreciation rates for each class. MACRS ignores salvage value.

The MACRS depreciation rates are used to determine the depreciation expense for taxable income, while other depreciation methods are used to arrive at the depreciation expense for net income. Since these depreciation methods have differing results, there will be a temporary difference between the book values of fixed assets under the two methods, which will gradually be resolved over their useful lives.

Accounting for Leasehold Improvements

Many veterinary practices lease space from a third party, and then pay to build out the property with walls, air conditioning, telephone wiring, and related permanent fixtures. These improvements are known as leasehold improvements. In accounting, a leasehold improvement is considered an asset of the tenant if the tenant paid for it, the investment exceeds the capitalization limit of the tenant, and the improvements will be usable for more than one reporting period. If so, you (the tenant) record the investment as a fixed asset and amortize it over the lesser of the remaining term of the lease or the useful life of the improvements. Upon the termination of the lease, all leasehold improvements become the property of the landlord.

Depreciation Accounting Entries

The basic depreciation entry is to debit the depreciation expense account (which appears in the income statement) and credit the accumulated depreciation account (which appears in the balance sheet as an account that reduces the amount of fixed assets). Over time, the accumulated depreciation balance will continue to increase as more depreciation is added to it, until such time as it equals the original cost of the asset. At that time, stop recording any depreciation expense, since the cost of the asset has now been reduced to zero.

The journal entry for depreciation can be a simple two-line entry designed to accommodate all types of fixed assets, or it may be subdivided into separate entries for each type of fixed asset.

EXAMPLE

Pembroke Veterinary calculates that it should have $25,000 of depreciation expense in the current month. The entry is:

	Debit	Credit
Depreciation expense	25,000	
Accumulated depreciation		25,000

In the following month, Pembroke's bookkeeper decides to show a higher level of precision at the expense account level, and instead elects to apportion the $25,000 of depreciation among different expense accounts, so that each class of asset has a separate depreciation charge. The entry is:

	Debit	Credit
Depreciation expense – Automobiles	4,000	
Depreciation expense – Computer equipment	8,000	
Depreciation expense – Furniture and fixtures	6,000	
Depreciation expense – Office equipment	5,000	
Depreciation expense – Software	2,000	
Accumulated depreciation		25,000

The journal entry to record the amortization of intangible assets is fundamentally the same as the entry for depreciation, except that the accounts used substitute the word "amortization" for depreciation.

EXAMPLE

Pembroke Veterinary calculates that it should have $4,000 of amortization expense in the current month that is related to intangible assets. The entry is:

	Debit	Credit
Amortization expense	4,000	
Accumulated amortization		4,000

Accumulated Depreciation

When you sell or otherwise dispose of an asset, remove all related accumulated depreciation from the accounting records at the same time. Otherwise, an unusually large amount of accumulated depreciation will build up on the balance sheet.

EXAMPLE

Penn Central Veterinary has $1,000,000 of fixed assets, for which it has charged $380,000 of accumulated depreciation. This results in the following presentation on Penn Central's balance sheet:

Fixed assets	$1,000,000
Less: Accumulated depreciation	(380,000)
Net fixed assets	$620,000

Penn Central then sells a diagnostic machine for $80,000 that had an original cost of $140,000, and for which it had already recorded accumulated depreciation of $50,000. It records the sale with this journal entry:

	Debit	Credit
Cash	80,000	
Accumulated depreciation	50,000	
Loss on asset sale	10,000	
Fixed assets		140,000

As a result of this entry, Penn Central's balance sheet presentation of fixed assets has changed, so that fixed assets before accumulated depreciation have declined to $860,000, and accumulated depreciation has declined to $330,000. The new presentation is:

Fixed assets	$860,000
Less: Accumulated depreciation	(330,000)
Net fixed assets	$530,000

The amount of net fixed assets declined by $90,000 as a result of the asset sale, which is the sum of the $80,000 cash proceeds and the $10,000 loss resulting from the asset sale.

Asset Disposal Accounting

There are two scenarios under which you may dispose of a fixed asset. The first situation arises when a fixed asset is being eliminated without receiving any payment in return. This is a common situation when a fixed asset is being scrapped because it is obsolete or no longer in use, and there is no resale market for it. In this case, reverse any accumulated depreciation and reverse the original asset cost. If the asset is fully depreciated, that is the extent of the entry.

EXAMPLE

Bradbury Veterinary buys a diagnostic machine for $100,000 and recognizes $10,000 of depreciation per year over the following ten years. At that time, the machine is not only fully depreciated, but also ready for the scrap heap. Bradbury gives away the machine for free, and records the following entry.

	Debit	Credit
Accumulated depreciation	100,000	
Machine asset		100,000

A variation on this situation is to write off a fixed asset that has not yet been completely depreciated. In this case, write off the remaining undepreciated amount of the asset to a loss account.

EXAMPLE

To use the same example, Bradbury Veterinary gives away the machine after eight years, when it has not yet depreciated $20,000 of the asset's original $100,000 cost. In this case, Bradbury records the following entry:

	Debit	Credit
Loss on asset disposal	20,000	
Accumulated depreciation	80,000	
Machine asset		100,000

The second scenario arises when an asset is sold, so that the firm receives cash in exchange for the asset. Depending upon the price paid and the remaining amount of depreciation that has not yet been charged to expense, this can result in either a gain or a loss on sale of the asset.

EXAMPLE

Bradbury Veterinary still disposes of its $100,000 machine, but does so after seven years, and sells it for $35,000 in cash. In this case, it has already recorded $70,000 of depreciation expense. The entry is:

	Debit	Credit
Cash	35,000	
Accumulated depreciation	70,000	
Gain on asset disposal		5,000
Machine asset		100,000

What if Bradbury had sold the machine for $25,000 instead of $35,000? Then there would be a loss of $5,000 on the sale. The entry would be:

	Debit	Credit
Cash	25,000	
Accumulated depreciation	70,000	
Loss on asset disposal	5,000	
Machine asset		100,000

The "loss on asset disposal" or "gain on asset disposal" accounts noted in the preceding sample entries are called disposal accounts. They may be combined into a single account or used separately to store gains and losses resulting from the disposal of fixed assets.

Accounting for the Cost of Goods Sold

The cost of goods sold for a veterinary practice includes clinical supplies and related costs. The amount of these costs incurred will vary directly with revenue, since more sales equates to more supply usage. However, the amount recorded will vary, depending on whether the business is operated under the cash basis of accounting or the accrual basis. Under the cash basis, supplies are charged to expense as soon as they are paid for, while supplies are charged to expense under the accrual basis only when they have been used. This can result in a lumpy expense recognition under the cash basis, especially when large amounts of supplies are purchased at the same time. Over the long term, these differences in timing will even out, but there can be notable differences over the short term.

Accounting for Payroll Transactions

There are several types of journal entries that involve the recordation of compensation. The primary entry is for the initial recordation of a payroll. This entry records the gross wages earned by employees, as well as all withholdings from their pay, and any additional taxes owed by the veterinary practice. There may also be an accrued wages entry that is recorded at the end of each accounting period, and which is intended to record the amount of wages owed to employees but not yet paid. Each of these types of compensation is based on different source documents and requires separate calculations and journal entries.

There are also a number of other payroll-related journal entries that a bookkeeper must deal with on a regular basis. They include:

- Accrued bonuses
- Manual paychecks
- Employee advances
- Accrued vacation pay
- Tax deposits

All of these journal entries are described in the following subsections.

Primary Payroll Journal Entry

The primary journal entry for payroll is the summary-level entry that is compiled from the payroll register, and which is recorded in either the payroll journal or the general ledger. This entry usually includes debits for the direct labor expense, wages, and the firm's portion of payroll taxes. There will also be credits to a number of other accounts, each one detailing the liability for payroll taxes that have not been paid, as well as for the amount of cash already paid to employees for their net pay. The basic entry (assuming no further breakdown of debits by individual profit center) appears in the following exhibit.

Sample Payroll Journal Entry

	Debit	Credit
Direct labor expense	xxx	
Wages expense	xxx	
Payroll taxes expense	xxx	
Cash		xxx
Federal withholding taxes payable		xxx
Social security taxes payable		xxx
Medicare taxes payable		xxx
Federal unemployment taxes payable		xxx
State unemployment taxes payable		xxx
Garnishments payable		xxx

The reason for the payroll taxes expense line item in this journal entry is that the practice incurs the cost of matching the social security and Medicare amounts paid by employees, and directly incurs the cost of unemployment insurance. The employee-paid portions of the social security and Medicare taxes are not recorded as expenses; instead, they are liabilities for which the firm has an obligation to remit cash to the taxing government entity.

A key point with this journal entry is that the direct labor expense and salaries expense contain employee gross pay, while the amount actually paid to employees through the cash account is their net pay. The difference between the two figures (which can be substantial) is the amount of deductions from their pay, such as payroll taxes and withholdings to pay for benefits.

There may be a number of additional employee deductions to include in this journal entry. For example, there may be deductions for 401(k) pension plans, health insurance, life insurance, vision insurance, and for the repayment of advances.

When the withheld taxes and company portion of payroll taxes are paid on a later date, use the entry format in the following exhibit to reduce the balance in the cash account, and eliminate the balances in the liability accounts.

Sample Journal Entry for Payroll Tax Payments

	Debit	Credit
Federal withholding taxes payable	xxx	
Social security taxes payable	xxx	
Medicare taxes payable	xxx	
Federal unemployment taxes payable	xxx	
State withholding taxes payable	xxx	
State unemployment taxes payable	xxx	
Garnishments payable	xxx	
Cash		xxx

Thus, when a veterinary practice initially deducts taxes and other items from an employee's pay, the firm incurs a liability to pay the taxes to a third party. This liability only disappears from its accounting records when it pays the related funds to the entity to which they are owed.

Accrued Wages

It is quite common to have some amount of unpaid wages at the end of an accounting period, so accrue this expense (if it is material). The accrual entry, as shown next, is simpler than the comprehensive payroll entry already shown, because all payroll taxes are typically clumped into a single expense account and offsetting liability account. After recording this entry, reverse it at the beginning of the following accounting period, and then record the actual payroll expense whenever it occurs.

Sample Accrued Wages Entry

	Debit	Credit
Direct labor expense	xxx	
Wages expense	xxx	
Accrued salaries and wages		xxx
Accrued payroll taxes		xxx

Veterinary practices with predominantly salaried staffs frequently avoid making the accrued wages entry, on the grounds that the wages due to a small number of hourly personnel at the end of the reporting period have a minimal impact on reported financial results.

The information for the wage accrual entry is most easily derived from a spreadsheet that itemizes all employees to whom the calculation applies, the amount of unpaid time, and the standard pay rate for each person. It is not necessary to also calculate the cost of overtime hours earned during an accrual period if the amount of such hours is relatively small. A sample spreadsheet for calculating accrued wages appears in the following exhibit.

Sample Accrued Wages Calculation

Hourly Employees	Unpaid Days	Hourly Rate	Pay Accrual
Anthem, Jill	4	$40.00	$1,280
Bingley, Adam	4	38.25	1,224
Chesterton, Elvis	4	37.50	1,200
Davis, Ethel	4	43.00	1,376
Ellings, Humphrey	4	41.50	1,328
Fogarty, Miriam	4	26.00	832
		Total	$7,240

Accrued Bonuses

Accrue a bonus expense whenever there is an expectation that the financial or operational performance of the practice at least equals the performance levels required in any active bonus plans.

The decision to accrue a bonus calls for considerable judgment, for the entire period of performance may encompass many future months, during which time a person may *not* continue to achieve his bonus plan objectives, in which case any prior bonus accrual should be reversed. Here are some alternative ways to treat a bonus accrual during the earlier stages of a bonus period:

- Accrue no expense at all until there is a reasonable probability that the bonus will be achieved.

34

- Accrue a smaller expense early in a performance period to reflect the higher risk of performance failure, and accrue a larger expense later if the probability of success improves.

One thing *not* to do is to accrue a significant bonus expense in a situation where the probability that the bonus will be awarded is low; such an accrual is essentially earnings management, since it creates a false expense that is later reversed when the performance period is complete.

EXAMPLE

The management team of Hiram Veterinarians will earn a year-end group bonus of $24,000 if profits exceed 12 percent of revenues. There is a reasonable probability that the team will earn this bonus, so the bookkeeper records the following accrual in each month of the performance year:

	Debit	Credit
Bonus expense	2,000	
Accrued bonus liability		2,000

The management team does not quite meet the profit criteria required under the bonus plan, so the group instead receives a $15,000 bonus. This results in the following entry to eliminate the liability and pay out the bonus:

	Debit	Credit
Accrued bonus liability	24,000	
Bonus expense		9,000
Cash		15,000

The actual payout of $15,000 would be reduced by any social security and Medicare taxes applicable to each person in the management group being paid.

Manual Paycheck Entry

It is all too common to create a manual paycheck, either because an employee was short-paid in a prior payroll, or because the practice is laying off or firing an employee, and so is obligated to pay that person before the next regularly scheduled payroll. This check may be paid through the practice's accounts payable bank account, rather than its payroll account, so you may need to make this entry through the accounts payable system.

EXAMPLE

Elderly Veterinarians lays off Mr. Jones. Elderly owes Mr. Jones $5,000 of wages at the time of the layoff. The bookkeeper calculates that she must withhold $382.50 from Mr. Jones' pay to cover the employee-paid portions of social security and Medicare taxes. Mr. Jones has claimed a large enough number of withholding allowances that there is no income tax withholding. Thus, the bookkeeper pays Mr. Jones $4,617.50. The journal entry used is:

	Debit	Credit
Wage expense	5,000	
Social security taxes payable		310.00
Medicare taxes payable		72.50
Cash		4,617.50

At the next regularly-scheduled payroll, the bookkeeper records this payment as a notation in the payroll system, so that it will properly compile the correct amount of wages for Mr. Jones for his year-end Form W-2. In addition, the payroll system calculates that Elderly must pay a matching amount of social security and Medicare taxes (though no unemployment taxes, since Mr. Jones already exceeded his wage cap for these taxes). Accordingly, an additional liability of $382.50 is recorded in the payroll journal entry for that payroll. Elderly pays these matching amounts as part of its normal tax remittances associated with the payroll.

Employee Advances

When an employee asks for an advance, this is recorded as a current asset in the firm's balance sheet. There may not be a separate account in which to store advances, especially if employee advances are infrequent; possible asset accounts that can be used are:

- Employee advances (for high-volume situations)
- Other assets (probably sufficient for smaller practices that record few assets other than trade receivables, inventory, and fixed assets)
- Other receivables (useful if management is tracking a number of different types of assets, and wants to segregate receivables in one account)

EXAMPLE

Frogmorton Veterinarians issues a $1,000 advance to employee Wes Smith. The bookkeeper issues advances regularly, and so uses a separate account in which to record advances. She records the transaction as:

	Debit	Credit
Other assets	1,000	
Cash		1,000

One week later, Mr. Smith pays back half the amount of the advance, which is recorded with this entry:

	Debit	Credit
Cash	500	
Other assets		500

No matter what method is later used to repay the practice – a check from the employee, or payroll deductions – the entry will be a credit to whichever asset account was used, until such time as the balance in the account has been paid off.

Accrued Vacation Pay

Accrued vacation pay is the amount of vacation time that an employee has earned as per a firm's employee benefit manual, but which he has not yet used. The calculation of accrued vacation pay for each employee is:

1. Calculate the amount of vacation time earned through the beginning of the accounting period. This should be a roll-forward balance from the preceding period.
2. Add the number of hours earned in the current accounting period.
3. Subtract the number of vacation hours used in the current period.
4. Multiply the ending number of accrued vacation hours by the employee's hourly wage to arrive at the correct accrual that should be on the firm's books.
5. If the amount already accrued for the employee from the preceding period is lower than the correct accrual, record the difference as an addition to the accrued liability. If the amount already accrued from the preceding period is higher than the correct accrual, record the difference as a reduction of the accrued liability.

A sample spreadsheet follows that uses the preceding steps, and which can be used to compile accrued vacation pay.

Sample Accrued Vacation Spreadsheet

Name	Vacation Roll-Forward Balance	+ New Hours Earned	- Hours Used	= Net Balance	× Hourly Pay	= Accrued Vacation $
Hilton, David	24.0	10	34.0	0.0	$35.00	$0.00
Idle, John	13.5	10	0.0	23.5	27.50	646.25
Jakes, Jill	120.0	10	80.0	50.0	43.50	2,175.00
Kilo, Steve	114.5	10	14.0	110.5	40.00	4,420.00
Linder, Alice	12.0	10	0.0	22.0	35.75	786.50
Mills, Jeffery	83.5	10	65.00	28.5	29.75	847.88
					Total	$8,875.63

It is not necessary to reverse the vacation pay accrual in each period if the decision is made to instead record just incremental changes in the accrual from month to month.

EXAMPLE

There is already an existing accrued balance of 40 hours of unused vacation time for Wes Smith on the books of Kimber Veterinarians. In the most recent month that has just ended, Mr. Smith accrued an additional five hours of vacation time (since he is entitled to 60 hours of accrued vacation time per year, and 60 ÷ 12 = five hours per month). He also used three hours of vacation time during the month. This means that, as of the end of the month, the bookkeeper should have accrued a total of 42 hours of vacation time for him (calculated as 40 hours existing balance + 5 hours additional accrual – 3 hours used).

Mr. Smith is paid $30 per hour, so his total vacation accrual should be $1,260 (42 hours × $30/hour), so the bookkeeper accrues an additional $60 of vacation liability.

What if a veterinary practice has a "use it or lose it" policy? This means that employees must use their vacation time by a certain date (such as the end of the year), and can only carry forward a small number of hours (if any) into the next year. One issue is that this policy may be illegal, since vacation is an earned benefit that cannot be taken away (which depends on state law). If this policy is considered to be legal, it is acceptable to reduce the accrual as of the date when employees are supposed to have used their accrued vacation, thereby reflecting the reduced liability to the firm as represented by the number of vacation hours that employees have lost.

What if an employee receives a pay raise? Then increase the amount of his entire vacation accrual by the incremental amount of the pay raise. This is because, if the employee were to leave the practice and be paid all of his unused vacation pay, he would be paid at his most recent rate of pay.

Tax Deposits

When an employer withholds taxes from employee pay, it must deposit these funds with the government at stated intervals. The journal entry for doing so is a debit to the tax liability account being paid and a credit to the cash account, which reduces the cash balance. For example, if a veterinary practice were to pay a state government for unemployment taxes, the entry would be:

	Debit	Credit
State unemployment taxes payable	xxx	
Cash		xxx

Closing the Books

The concept of closing the books refers to summarizing the information in the accounting records into the financial statements at the end of a reporting period. In this section, we give an overview of closing journal entries and the most prevalent closing activities that a veterinary practice is likely to need.

The Accruals Concept

An accrual allows you to record expenses and revenues for which you expect to expend cash or receive cash, respectively, in a future reporting period. The offset to an accrued expense is an accrued liability account, which appears in the balance sheet. The offset to accrued revenue is an accrued asset account (such as unbilled fees), which also appears in the balance sheet. Examples of accruals are:

- *Revenue accrual.* A practice's boarding group will eventually bill a client for $2,000. It can record an accrual in the current period so that its current income statement shows $2,000 of revenue, even though it has not yet billed the client.
- *Expense accrual – interest.* A veterinary practice has a loan with the local bank for $1 million, and pays interest on the loan at a variable rate of interest. The invoice from the bank for $3,000 in interest expense does not arrive until the following month, so the firm accrues the expense in order to show the amount on its income statement in the proper month.
- *Expense accrual – wages.* A practice pays its employees at the end of each month for their hours worked through the 25th day of the month. To fully record the wage expense for the entire month, it also accrues $12,000 in additional wages, which represents the cost of wages for the remaining days of the month.

Most accruals are initially created as reversing entries, so that the accounting software automatically cancels them in the following month. This happens when you are expecting revenue to actually be billed, or supplier invoices to actually arrive, in the next month. The concept is addressed later in the Reversing Entries sub-section.

Adjusting Entries

Adjusting entries are journal entries that are used at the end of an accounting period to adjust the balances in various general ledger accounts to more closely align the reported results and financial position of a business to meet the requirements of an accounting framework, such as Generally Accepted Accounting Principles.

An adjusting entry can be used for any type of accounting transaction; here are some of the more common ones:

- To record depreciation
- To record an allowance for doubtful accounts
- To record accrued revenue
- To record accrued expenses
- To record previously paid but unused expenditures as prepaid expenses
- To adjust cash balances for any reconciling items noted in the bank reconciliation

Adjusting entries are most commonly of three types, which are:

- *Accruals*. To record a revenue or expense that has not yet been recorded through a standard accounting transaction.
- *Deferrals*. To defer a revenue or expense that has occurred, but which has not yet been earned or used.
- *Estimates*. To estimate the amount of a reserve, such as the allowance for doubtful accounts.

When a journal entry is recorded for an accrual, deferral, or estimate, it usually impacts an asset or liability account. For example, if an expense is accrued, this also increases a liability account. Or, if revenue recognition is deferred to a later period, this also increases a liability account. Thus, adjusting entries impact the balance sheet, not just the income statement.

Reversing Entries

When a journal entry is created, it may be to record revenue or an expense other than through a more traditional method, such as issuing an invoice to a customer or recording an invoice from a supplier. In these situations, the journal entry is only meant to be a stopgap measure, with the traditional recordation method still being used at a later date. This means that the bookkeeper has to eventually create a journal entry that is the *opposite* of the original entry, thereby cancelling out the original entry. The concept is best explained with an example.

EXAMPLE

The bookkeeper of Archimedes Veterinary has not yet received an invoice from a key supplier of vaccines by the time he closes the books for the month of May. He expects that the invoice will be for $2,000, so he records the following accrual entry for the invoice:

	Debit	Credit
Vaccines expense	2,000	
Accrued expenses		2,000

This entry creates an additional expense of $2,000 for the month of May.

The bookkeeper knows that the invoice will arrive in June and will be recorded upon receipt. Therefore, he creates a reversing entry for the original accrual in early June that cancels out the original entry. The entry is:

	Debit	Credit
Accrued expenses	2,000	
Vaccines expense		2,000

The invoice then arrives, and is recorded in the normal manner through the accounts payable module in Archimedes' accounting software. This creates an expense during the month of June of $2,000. Thus, the net effect in June is:

June reversing entry	-$2,000
Supplier invoice	+2,000
Net effect in June	$0

In short, the accrual entry shifts recognition of the expense from June to May.

Any accounting software package contains an option for automatically creating a reversing journal entry when a journal entry is initially set up. Always use this feature when a reversing entry will be needed. By doing so, you can avoid the risk of forgetting to manually create the reversing entry, and also avoid the risk of creating an incorrect entry.

> **Tip:** There will be situations where there is no expectation to reverse a journal entry for a few months. If so, consider using an automated reversing entry in the *next* month, and creating a replacement journal entry in each successive month. While this approach may appear time-consuming, it ensures that the original entry is *always* flushed from the books, thereby avoiding the risk of carrying a journal entry past the date when it should have been eliminated.

Common Adjusting Entries

This section contains a discussion of the journal entries that a veterinary practice is most likely to need to close the books, along with an example of the accounts most likely to be used in the entries.

Depreciation

This entry is used to gradually charge the investment in fixed assets to expense over the useful lives of those assets. The amount of depreciation is calculated from a spreadsheet or fixed asset software, and is based on a systematic method for spreading recognition of the expense over multiple periods.

Allowance for Doubtful Accounts

If a business sells goods or services on credit, there is a strong likelihood that a portion of the resulting accounts receivable will eventually become bad debts. If so, update the allowance for doubtful accounts each month. This account offsets the balance in the accounts receivable account. Set the balance in this allowance to match the best estimate of how much of the month-end accounts receivable will eventually be written off as bad debts. A sample entry is:

	Debit	Credit
Bad debts expense	xxx	
Allowance for doubtful accounts		xxx

Accrued Revenue

If a practice has engaged in work for a client but has not yet billed the client, it may be possible to recognize some or all of the revenue associated with the work performed to date. The offset to the revenue is a debit to an accrued accounts receivable account. Do not record this accrual in the standard trade accounts receivable account, since that account should be reserved for actual billings. A sample of the accrued revenue entry is:

	Debit	Credit
Accounts receivable – accrued	xxx	
Sales		xxx

42

It is also possible for the reverse situation to arise, where a client is invoiced in advance of completing work on the billed items. In this case, *reduce* recorded sales by the amount of unearned revenue by crediting an unearned sales (liability) account. A sample entry is:

	Debit	Credit
Sales	xxx	
Unearned sales (liability)		xxx

Accrued Expenses

If there are supplier invoices that you are aware of but have not yet received, estimate the amount of the expense and accrue it with a journal entry. There are any number of expense accounts to which such transactions might be charged; in the following sample entry, we assume that the expense relates to a supplier invoice for utilities that has not yet arrived.

	Debit	Credit
Utilities expense	xxx	
Accrued expenses		xxx

This is likely to be the most frequent of the adjusting entries, as there may be a number of supplier invoices that do not arrive by the time a practice officially closes its books.

Prepaid Assets

Occasionally, a veterinary practice will make a significant payment in advance to a third party. This advance may be for something that will be charged to expense in a later period, or it may be a deposit that will be returned at a later date. These payments should initially be recorded as assets, usually in the prepaid assets account. Situations where one may record a prepaid asset include:

- Rent paid before the month to which it applies
- Medical insurance paid before the month to which it applies
- Rent deposit, to be returned at the conclusion of a lease
- Utilities deposit, to be retained until the organization cancels service

Most of these transactions have the same journal entry, which is:

	Debit	Credit
Prepaid expenses	xxx	
Cash		xxx

The name of the debited account can vary. We use "Prepaid expenses" in the sample entry, but "Prepaid assets" is also used.

Update Reserves

If the organization is using the accrual basis of accounting, create a reserve in the expectation that expenses will be incurred in the future that are related to revenues generated now. This concept is called the matching principle. Under the matching principle, record the cause and effect of a business transaction at the same time. Thus, when revenue is recorded, also record within the same accounting period any expenses directly related to that revenue. An example of this type of expense is the allowance for doubtful accounts; this allowance is used to charge to expense the amount of bad debts that are expected from a certain amount of sales, before you know precisely which items will not be paid.

There is no need to create a reserve if the balance in the account is going to be immaterial. Instead, many businesses can generate perfectly adequate financial statements that only have a few reserves, while charging all other expenditures to expense as incurred.

Reconcile the Bank Statement

The bank reconciliation matches the amount of cash recorded by the veterinary practice to what its bank has recorded. Once a bank reconciliation has been constructed, you can have considerable confidence that the amount of cash appearing on the balance sheet is correct.

At a minimum, conduct a bank reconciliation shortly after the end of each month, when the bank sends a bank statement containing the bank's beginning cash balance, transactions during the month, and its ending cash balance. It is even better to conduct a bank reconciliation every day based on the bank's month-to-date information, which should be accessible on the bank's web site. By completing a daily bank reconciliation, problems can be spotted and corrected immediately.

A likely outcome of the reconciliation process will be several adjustments to a practice's recorded cash balance. It is unlikely that the firm's ending cash balance and the bank's ending cash balance will be identical, since there are probably multiple payments and deposits in transit at all times, as well as bank service fees, penalties, and not sufficient funds deposits that the practice has not yet recorded.

The essential process flow for a bank reconciliation is to start with the bank's ending cash balance (known as the *bank balance*), add to it any deposits in transit from the practice to the bank, subtract any checks that have not yet cleared the bank, and either add or deduct any other reconciling items. Then find the firm's ending cash balance and deduct from it any bank service fees, not sufficient funds (NSF) checks and penalties, and add to it any interest earned. At the end of this process, the adjusted bank balance should equal the firm's ending adjusted cash balance.

The following bank reconciliation procedure assumes that the bank reconciliation is being created in an accounting software package, which makes the reconciliation process easier:

1. Enter the bank reconciliation software module. A listing of uncleared checks and uncleared deposits will appear.
2. Check off in the bank reconciliation module all checks that are listed on the bank statement as having cleared the bank.
3. Check off in the bank reconciliation module all deposits that are listed on the bank statement as having cleared the bank.
4. Enter as expenses all bank charges appearing on the bank statement, and which have not already been recorded in the practice's records.
5. Enter the ending balance on the bank statement. If the book and bank balances match, then post all changes recorded in the bank reconciliation, and close the module. If the balances do *not* match, then continue reviewing the bank reconciliation for additional reconciling items. Look for the following items:

   - Checks recorded in the bank records at a different amount from what is recorded in the firm's records.
   - Deposits recorded in the bank records at a different amount from what is recorded in the firm's records.
   - Checks recorded in the bank records that are not recorded at all in the firm's records.
   - Deposits recorded in the bank records that are not recorded at all in the firm's records.
   - Inbound wire transfers from which a processing fee has been extracted.

EXAMPLE

Simple Veterinarians is closing its books for the month ended April 30. Simple's bookkeeper must prepare a bank reconciliation based on the following issues:

1. The bank statement contains an ending bank balance of $320,000.
2. The bank statement contains a $200 check printing charge for new checks that the practice ordered.
3. The bank statement contains a $150 service charge for operating the bank account.
4. The bank rejected a deposit of $500 due to not sufficient funds, and charges the firm a $10 fee associated with the rejection.
5. The bank statement contains interest income of $30.
6. Simple issued $80,000 of checks that have not yet cleared the bank.
7. Simple deposited $25,000 of checks at month-end that were not deposited in time to appear on the bank statement.

The bookkeeper creates the following reconciliation:

		Item #	Adjustment to Books
Bank balance	$320,000	1	
- Check printing charge	-200	2	Debit expense, credit cash
- Service charge	-150	3	Debit expense, credit cash
- NSF fee	-10	4	Debit expense, credit cash
- NSF deposit rejected	-500	4	Debit receivable, credit cash
+ Interest income	+30	5	Debit cash, credit interest income
- Uncleared checks	-80,000	6	None
+ Deposits in transit	+25,000	7	None
= Book balance	$264,170		

When the bank reconciliation process is complete, print a report through the accounting software that shows the bank and book balances, the identified differences between the two (most likely to be uncleared checks), and any remaining unreconciled difference.

The format of the report will vary by software package; a simplistic layout follows.

Sample Bank Reconciliation Statement

For the month ended March 31, 20x3		
Bank balance	$850,000	
Less: Checks outstanding	-225,000	See detail
Add: Deposits in transit	+100,000	See detail
+/- Other adjustments	0	
Book balance	$725,000	
Unreconciled difference	$0	

There are several problems that continually arise as part of a bank reconciliation. They are:

- *Uncleared checks that continue to not be presented.* There will be a residual number of checks that either are not presented to the bank for payment for a long time, or which are never presented for payment. In the short term, treat them in the same manner as any other uncleared checks - just keep them in the uncleared checks listing in the accounting software, so they will be an ongoing reconciling item. In the long term, contact the payee to see if they ever received the check; it will likely be necessary to void the old check and issue them a new one.

- *Checks clear the bank after having been voided*. As just noted, if a check remains uncleared for a long time, the old check will likely be voided and replaced with a new check. But what if the payee then cashes the original check? If it was voided with the bank, the bank should reject the check when it is presented. If the bookkeeper did *not* void it with the bank, then record the check again in the accounting records, which will reduce the cash balance. If the payee has not yet cashed the replacement check, void it with the bank at once to avoid a double payment. Otherwise, it will be necessary to pursue repayment of the second check by the payee.
- *Deposited checks are returned*. There are cases where the bank will refuse to deposit a check, usually because it is drawn on a bank account located in another country. In this case, reverse the original entry related to that deposit, which will reduce the cash balance.

Calculate Depreciation

Once all fixed assets have been recorded in the accounting records for the month, calculate the amount of depreciation (for tangible assets) and amortization (for intangible assets). We covered the calculation of depreciation earlier in this book.

Record All Payables

Accounts payable can be a significant bottleneck in the closing process. The reason is that some suppliers only issue invoices at the end of each month when they are closing *their* books, so the practice will not receive their invoices until several days into the next month. This circumstance usually arises either when a supplier ships something near the end of the month or when it is providing a continuing service. There are several choices for dealing with these items:

1. *Do nothing*. By waiting a few days, the invoices will arrive in the mail, and you can record the invoices and close the books. The advantage of this approach is a high degree of precision and perfect supporting evidence for all expenses. The downside is that it can significantly delay the issuance of financial statements.
2. *Accrue continuing service items*. As just noted, suppliers providing continuing services are more likely to issue invoices at month-end. When services are being provided on a continuing basis, you can easily estimate what the expense should be, based on prior invoices. Thus, it is not difficult to create reversing journal entries for these items at the end of the month. It is likely that these accruals will vary somewhat from the amounts on the actual invoices, but the differences should be immaterial.
3. *Accrue based on purchase orders*. As just noted, suppliers issue invoices at month-end when they ship goods near that date. If the practice is using purchase orders to order these items, the supplier is supposed to issue an invoice containing the same price stated on the purchase order. Therefore, if an item is received at the receiving dock but there is no accompanying invoice, use

the purchase order to create a reversing journal entry that accrues the expense associated with the received item.

In short, we strongly recommend using accruals to record expenses for supplier invoices that have not yet arrived. The sole exception is the end of the fiscal year, when the outside auditors may expect a greater degree of precision and supporting evidence, and will expect the bookkeeper to wait for actual invoices to arrive before closing the books.

Reconcile Accounts

It is important to examine the contents of the balance sheet accounts to verify that the recorded assets and liabilities are supposed to be there. It is quite possible that some items are still listed in an account that should have been flushed out a long time ago, which can be quite embarrassing if they are still on record when the auditors review the company's books at the end of the year. Here are several situations that a proper account reconciliation would have caught:

- *Prepaid assets.* An organization pays $10,000 to an insurance company as an advance on its regular monthly medical insurance, and records the payment as a prepaid asset. The asset lingers on the books until year-end, when the auditors inquire about it, and the full amount is then charged to expense.
- *Accrued revenue.* A veterinary practice accrues revenue of $5,000 for a surgery, but forgets to reverse the entry in the following month, when it invoices the full $5,000 to the client. This results in the double recordation of revenue, which is not spotted until year-end. The bookkeeper then reverses the accrual, thereby unexpectedly reducing revenues for the full year by $5,000.
- *Depreciation.* A veterinary practice calculates the depreciation on many assets with an electronic spreadsheet, which unfortunately does not track when to stop depreciating assets. A year-end review finds that the organization charged $40,000 of excess depreciation to expense.
- *Accumulated depreciation.* A veterinary practice has been disposing of its assets for years, but has never bothered to eliminate the associated accumulated depreciation from its balance sheet. Doing so reduces both the fixed asset and accumulated depreciation accounts by 50%.
- *Accounts payable.* A veterinary practice does not compare its accounts payable detail report to the general ledger account balance, which is $8,000 lower than the detail. The auditors spot the error and require a correcting entry at year-end, so that the account balance matches the detail report.

These issues and many more are common problems encountered at year-end. To prevent the extensive error corrections caused by these problems, conduct account reconciliations every month for the larger accounts, and occasionally review the detail for the smaller accounts, too. The following exhibit contains some of the account reconciliations to conduct, as well as the specific issues for which to look.

Sample Account Reconciliation List

Account	Reconciliation Discussion
Cash	There can be a number of unrecorded checks, deposits, and bank fees that will only be spotted with a bank reconciliation. It is permissible to do a partial bank reconciliation a day or two before the close, but completely ignoring it is not a good idea.
Accounts receivable	The accounts receivable detail report should match the account balance. If not, a journal entry was probably created that should be eliminated from this account.
Prepaid assets	This account may contain a variety of assets that will be charged to expense in the short term, so it may require frequent reviews to ensure that items have been flushed out in a timely manner.
Fixed assets	It is quite likely that fixed assets will initially be recorded in the wrong fixed asset account, or that they are disposed of incorrectly. Reconcile the account to the fixed asset detail report at least once a quarter to spot and correct these issues.
Accumulated depreciation	The balance in this account may not match the fixed asset detail if you have not removed the accumulated depreciation from the account upon the sale or disposal of an asset. This is not a critical issue, but still warrants an occasional review.
Accounts payable	The accounts payable detail report should match the account balance. If not, a journal entry was probably included in the account, which should be reversed.
Accrued expenses	This account can include a large number of accruals for such expenses as wages, vacations, and benefits. It is good practice to reverse all of these expenses in the month following recordation. Thus, if there is a residual balance, there may be an excess accrual still on the books.
Notes payable	The balance in this account should exactly match the account balance of the lender, barring any exceptions for in-transit payments to the lender.

The number of accounts that can be reconciled makes it clear that this is one of the larger steps involved in closing the books. Selected reconciliations can be skipped from time to time, but doing so presents the risk of an error creeping into the financial statements and not being spotted for quite a few months. Consequently, there is a significant risk of issuing inaccurate financial statements if some reconciliations are continually avoided.

Review Financial Statements

Once all of the preceding steps have been completed, review the financial statements for errors. There are several ways to do so, including:

- *Horizontal analysis*. Print reports that show the income statement and balance sheet for the past twelve months on a rolling basis. Track across each line item to see if there are any unusual declines or spikes in comparison to the results of prior periods, and investigate those items. This is the best review technique.
- *Budget versus actual*. Print an income statement that shows budgeted versus actual results, and investigate any larger variances. This is a less effective review technique, because it assumes that the budget is realistic, and also because a budget is not usually available for the balance sheet.

There will almost always be problems with the first iteration of the financial statements. Expect to investigate and correct several items before issuing a satisfactory set of financials. To reduce the amount of time needed to review financial statement errors during the core closing period, consider doing so a few days prior to month-end; this may uncover a few errors, leaving a smaller number to investigate later on.

Accrue Tax Liabilities

Once the financial statements have been created and the information in them has been finalized, there may be a need to accrue an income tax liability based on the amount of net profit. There are several issues to consider when creating this accrual:

- *Income tax rate*. When accruing income taxes, use the average expected income tax rate for the full year.
- *Losses*. If the practice has earned a taxable profit in a prior period of the year, and has now generated a loss, accrue for a tax rebate, which will offset the tax expense that was recorded earlier. Doing so creates the correct amount of tax liability when looking at year-to-date results. If there was no prior profit and no reasonable prospect of one, do not accrue for a tax rebate, since it is more likely than not that the firm will not receive the rebate.

Once the income tax liability has been accrued, print the complete set of financial statements.

Close the Month

Once all transactions have been entered into the accounting system, close the month in the accounting software. This means prohibiting any further transactions in the general ledger in the old accounting period, as well as allowing the next accounting period to accept transactions. These steps are important, to avoid inadvertently entering transactions into the wrong accounting periods. Then issue the financial statements.

Veterinary Practice Financial Analysis

There are several ways to fine-tune the results being generated by a veterinary practice. In the following bullet points, we note a variety of analyses that can enhance your profitability:

- *Pricing analysis*. It can be useful to periodically compile the cost of each service provided, and compare this cost to the billing rate being charged to clients. If the cost of the labor or materials consumed is high, then be sure to charge a commensurately higher fee for these services. A useful time to conduct a pricing analysis is right after employees have been given pay raises, so that these added costs flow through to the pricing schedule.

- *Common sizing analysis*. Add a column to the income statement that shows each expense line item as a percentage of net revenues. This is useful for comparisons across years, to see if expenses have changed as a proportion of revenues. This is especially important when there has been a significant change to the practice, such as moving into a larger facility in order to add staff.

- *Staff revenue analysis*. Calculate the revenue being generated by each veterinarian. It is possible that some veterinarians are involved in lower-priced services that generate less total revenue, or are less efficient in using their time, and so see fewer patients. These issues can result in changes in the prices of services offered (in the first case), and the possible termination of veterinarians or adjustments to their compensation (in the second case).

- *Staff profit analysis*. It can be useful to develop a report for each revenue-generating employee, noting the revenue generated by each one, against which is offset their compensation, employer-paid payroll taxes, benefit costs, training, travel, and all other directly related expenses. This is a good way to see if the practice is generating a profit on each of its employees.

- *Overtime review*. It is easy for a veterinary practice to rack up substantial overtime expenses, especially when it offers extended operating hours. This is worth investigating in detail each month for actionable items. For example, if there is a substantial amount of overtime in every month, it may be time to hire more regular staff, or impose more draconian controls over the use of overtime.

Relevant Accounting Controls

A veterinary practice is just as likely to experience losses from fraud or incorrect accounting transactions as any other. Given its relatively small size and restricted range of accounting transactions, this limits the need for offsetting controls to a few key areas, which we note in the following bullet points. Ensuring that these controls are in place and actively maintained can significantly decrease your risk of loss.

General Controls

- *Segregate duties*. The typical veterinary practice is relatively small, with just a few administrative staff. This results in an unfortunate concentration of accounting tasks with one or two people. When this is the case, it is much easier for someone to steal funds from the business and cover their tracks. Segregating duties is the answer. For example, have one person open the mail to extract check payments, who passes them along to someone else who records them, while another person fills out a deposit slip before the money is sent to the bank. Yet another person conducts the monthly bank reconciliation, to cross-check what was received. By spreading these tasks among several people, it is difficult for someone to remove cash from the system without a trace.

- *Switch accounting tasks*. Cross-train several people in the basic accounting functions, and then have them rotate jobs from time to time. Doing so should uncover any instances of theft that require the same person to cover up the evidence of a crime for an extended period of time.
- *Mandate vacations*. Force employees to take the vacation time that they have earned, rather than continually carrying it forward. Doing so keeps them out of the office, so they are unable to cover up any ongoing scams in which they might be engaged.
- *Conduct a bank reconciliation*. A good way to spot issues is to complete a bank reconciliation for every open bank account. Better yet, conduct reconciliations at odd intervals, rather than just at the end of the month. Doing so is a good way to catch discrepancies.
- *Conduct a review*. Have an outside auditor examine the firm's accounting practices. Doing so may not only uncover discrepancies, but also cases in which controls may be added or modified.

Cash Receipt Controls

- *Open the mail and record cash receipts*. Someone not otherwise involved in the handling or recordation of cash receipts opens the mail, records all cash and checks received, and then forwards the cash receipts to the cashier. To strengthen this control, have two people jointly open the mail.
- *Endorse for deposit only*. The person opening the mail should also immediately endorse all checks received with a "For Deposit Only" stamp, preferably one that also lists the practice's bank account number. This makes it much more difficult for someone to extract a check and deposit it into some other account.
- *Direct payments to lockbox*. An excellent control is to set up a lockbox at a bank, and direct customers to send their payments directly to the bank. This eliminates all risk of cash or checks being stolen from within the practice, and may also accelerate the recognition of cash in the firm's bank account by a day or so.
- *Apply cash at once*. There are several reasons why the cashier should apply cash to customer accounts as soon as the cash is received. First, it removes overdue accounts receivable from the aged receivables report, and therefore keeps the collection person from wasting time on collection calls. Also,

immediate cash application means that the cash will then be shifted off the premises and deposited, leaving little time for anyone to steal it.

- *Deposit daily.* If checks or cash are left on-site overnight, there is an increased chance that they may be stolen. To mitigate this risk, always deposit cash and checks at the end of every business day.
- *Lock up cash during transport.* Store all cash in a locked container while transporting it to the bank for deposit. This is not a good control, since some-one could steal the entire container. A better approach for transporting large amounts of cash is to hire an armored car company to transport the cash on behalf of the practice.
- *Match cash receipts journal to bank receipt.* When funds are deposited at the bank, the bank clerk hands over a receipt for the amount deposited. The per-son transporting the cash to the bank gives this receipt to the cashier, who compares it to the cash receipts journal. If the numbers do not match, it may mean that the person transporting the cash removed some cash prior to the deposit, though it may also mean that either the cashier or the bank incorrectly recorded the amount of cash.

Collection Controls

- *Mandate a collections procedure.* There should be a standard set of activities that the collections person is required to pursue when contacting customers about collection issues.
- *Require collections record keeping.* It is impossible to determine the status of an overdue account receivable unless the collections person maintains ade-quate records regarding the dates when contacts were made, promises made by clients, and next expected action dates.
- *Review collection actions taken.* The practice owner should hold regular meetings with the collections person to learn about collection actions taken, as well as expected payments. This is a useful control for ascertaining whether there have been lapses in collection activity.
- *Supervisory approval is needed to write off invoices.* The owner should ap-prove the write off of invoices requested by the collections person. This typi-cally involves a review of all collection actions taken thus far, to ensure that all necessary actions have been taken. It is also necessary to prevent collusion by the collections person with the cash receipts person, which could abscond with incoming client cash and then write off the related invoice.

Payables Controls

- *Approve invoices.* The person in a position to authorize payment signifies his or her approval of a supplier invoice.
- *Split check printing and signing.* One person should prepare checks, and a different person should sign them. By doing so, there is a cross-check on the issuance of cash.

- *Store all checks in a locked location.* Unused check stock should *always* be stored in a locked location. Otherwise, checks can be stolen and fraudulently filled out and cashed. This means that any signature plates or stamps should also be stored in a locked location.
- *Assign credit card responsibility.* The practice may very well use a procurement card to make any number of purchases. If so, assign responsibility for the card to just one person – no one else is allowed to use it. Further, you should review the monthly card statement to see if there are any unwarranted expenditures listed on it, and follow up with the responsible person.
- *Track the sequence of check numbers used.* Maintain a log in which are listed the range of check numbers used during a check run. This is useful for determining if any checks in storage might be missing. This log should not be kept with the stored checks, since someone could steal the log at the same time they steal checks.
- *Stamp invoices "paid".* In a purely manual payables environment, there is a risk of paying an invoice more than once, so a reasonable control is to stamp each paid invoice, or even perforate it with a "paid" stamp. This control is less necessary (if at all) in a computerized system, which automatically tracks which invoices have been paid.

Tip: Be especially careful to examine smaller charges on the practice's credit card. Someone might be running small personal items through the card, assuming that you will not notice.

- *Avoid using petty cash.* Petty cash is a small amount of cash kept on the premises to pay for incidentals or reimburse employees. This cash reserve is subject to theft, so it would be better not to use it at all, and instead employ a procurement card for smaller purchases.

Payroll Controls

- *Verify hours worked.* Have supervisors approve hours worked by their employees, to prevent the employees from charging more time than they actually worked.
- *Verify overtime worked.* Even if supervisors are not required to approve the hours worked by employees, at least have supervisors approve overtime hours worked. There is a pay premium associated with these hours, so the cost to the practice is higher, and is a temptation for employees to claim them.
- *Verify aggregation calculations.* If payroll is being calculated manually, have a second person verify the aggregation of hours worked. A second person is more likely to conduct a careful examination than the person who originated the calculations.
- *Match entered totals to timesheets.* If there has been a history of errors in entering timekeeping information into the payroll software, consider adding a control to match the entered totals to the aggregated totals listed on

employee timesheets. If automated timekeeping systems are in use, this information will be entered automatically, and no control is needed.

- *Review preliminary payroll register.* In a computerized system, the first evidence that the bookkeeper may have made a mistake will appear on the preliminary payroll register. A major control is to engage in as many iterations of this report as necessary, printing the register, looking for mistakes, correcting the mistakes, printing a replacement register, and so on.

- *Manager approves final payroll register.* Once all time information has been entered in the payroll system and wages and related deductions have been calculated, print a final payroll register that summarizes this information, and have a manager review and approve it.

- *Hand checks to employees.* Where possible, hand checks directly to employees. Doing so prevents a type of fraud where a bookkeeper creates a check for a ghost employee and pockets the check. A *ghost employee* is a fake employee record to which payments are fraudulently made. It could be an entirely fabricated person, or else a former employee whose record still indicates that he or she is an active employee.

- *Lock up undistributed checks.* If a practice does not distribute checks at once, they should be stored in a locked location. Otherwise, there is a risk of theft, with the person stealing the checks modifying them sufficiently to cash them.

- *Verify tax remittances.* The penalties associated with a late or missing tax remittance are severe, so have someone independently verify the amount of tax to remit, verify that the funds were actually sent to the government, and that the practice received a receipt in exchange.

> **Tip:** Outsourcing payroll processing eliminates the tax remittance problem, since the supplier is now responsible for it.

Budgeting Controls

- *Compare budget to actuals.* A budget is useless unless you compare it to actual results as part of the month-end financial statement review process. This means digging down into the accounting data to ascertain why actual revenues and expenses differed from the expectations stated in the budget. In addition, those responsible for each line item in the financial statements should make changes to ensure that actual results are aligned with the budget; the results of this activity should be reflected in their annual performance reviews.

Fraud Indicators

In a small veterinary practice, it is relatively easy to monitor employees. If you can do so, be watchful for the following characteristics, which can be indicative of someone who is engaged in fraud:

- *Hogs work.* Someone who is reluctant to hand over work to others might be engaged in fraudulent activities that would be uncovered if someone else were to look over their work.
- *Presents a disorganized front.* Someone might give the appearance of being disorganized, which is used as an excuse for incurring small losses that are actually intentional thefts of assets. Alternatively, the person might appear to make a number of mistakes on an ongoing basis, when these "mistakes" are really being used to cover up asset thefts.
- *Works extended hours.* If an employee is constantly in the office when no one else is, he or she might be using the extra time to adjust the accounting records to cover up cases of fraud.

A key issue for a veterinary practice is that the business is inherently rather small, which makes it difficult for someone to steal all that much without being noticed. Consequently, you need to search for smaller losses, perhaps $50 in one place and $30 somewhere else. Individually, these amounts are minor, but can add up to a substantial amount over a long period of time.

Cost Control

We have already noted the variety of analyses that can be used to spot revenue, expense, or profit anomalies. In addition, there are several managerial approaches to maintaining a reasonable level of control over incurred costs. One is to assign responsibility to someone for each profit center. By doing so, you can tie their performance (for compensation purposes) to how well their assigned profit center performs. For example, if your boarding operations are running at a loss, the person assigned responsibility for it should be examining all revenue and expense line items for it to determine why, while also formulating corrective actions.

> **Tip:** The person responsible for a profit center should be the only one allowed to authorize expenditures for it. Otherwise, it will be impossible to control costs for the profit center.

Another way to maintain control over costs is to develop a budget for each profit center, and regularly compare actual results to the budget. If you do this, be sure to devise a budget that is firmly grounded in reality (i.e., historical records), so that it can be considered a believable basis for comparison. If you see expenses diverging sharply from the budget, that is a strong indicator that you need to investigate further.

> **Tip:** Give the manager of each profit center responsibility for creating a budget for their area, so that you can hold them responsible for attaining the budget.

A budget is also a useful planning tool. You can use it not just to make a logical carryforward of this year's results into next year, but also to play with assumptions, such as the impact of adding another veterinarian, administrative person, profit center, or service offering. It might also reflect anticipated changes in your operations, such as alterations to working hours, the retirement of a veterinarian, or a change in your advertising methods.

Once a budget has been created, load the results into your accounting software. You can then have the system produce budget-versus-actual income statements, with automatically-calculated variances for each line item.

> **Tip:** A good cross-check on whether a budget can be achieved is to compare the initial budgeted revenue figure to the capacity of the business. If no veterinarians are being added and working hours are not being extended, then there is a good chance that an increase in budgeted revenues will not be achieved.

Summary

A veterinary practice has several characteristics that drive how its accounting systems should be structured. It has very few administrative staff, so accounting duties will need to be parceled out with care, to maximize the segregation of duties. Also, most of its services will be paid for on-site, resulting in a relatively small number of receivables; this places an emphasis on ensuring that the initial billing and cash receipt are absolutely correct. Another issue is the presence of a number of profit centers, each of which will require separate reporting to highlight whether any of them are having trouble generating a profit. And finally, the main expense of the practice is compensation, so the payroll process must be performed with great accuracy, to keep the staff happy.

Glossary

A

Accounts. The financial records of a business.

Accrual. A journal entry that is used to recognize revenues and expenses that have been earned or consumed, respectively, and for which the related source documents have not yet been received or generated.

Accrual basis of accounting. The concept of recording revenues when earned and expenses as incurred.

Asset. An expenditure that has utility through multiple future reporting periods.

B

Balance sheet. A report that shows a firm's total assets, liabilities, and owners' equity as of the final day of a reporting period.

C

Cash basis of accounting. A system of accounting under which revenues are recorded when cash is received, and expenses are recorded when cash is paid.

Credit. An accounting entry that either increases a liability or equity account, or decreases an asset or expense account.

D

Debit. An accounting entry that either increases an asset or expense account, or decreases a liability or equity account.

Depreciation. To charge to expense a portion of an asset that relates to the revenue generated by that asset.

Direct cost. Any cost that is only incurred in relation to an activity.

Double entry accounting. A record keeping system under which every transaction is recorded in at least two accounts.

E

Equity. The net amount of funds invested in a business by its owners, plus any earnings that have been retained within the business.

G

General ledger. A set of numbered accounts that a business uses to store its accounting transactions.

Ghost employee. A fake employee record to which payments are fraudulently made.

I

Income statement. A report that shows the revenue generated during a reporting period, from which all expenses incurred during that period are subtracted, leaving a profit or loss.

Indirect cost. Any cost that does not change with a change in activity.

L

Liability. A legally binding obligation payable to another entity.

M

Matching principle. The concept that revenues and all related expenses are to be recorded within the same reporting period.

P

Profit center. A department that generates revenues and profits or losses.

T

Transaction. A business event that has a monetary impact on a practice's financial statements, and is recorded as an entry in its accounting records.

U

Useful life. The time period over which it is expected that an asset will be productive.

Index

Account reconciliation........................... 48
Accounting controls.............................. 51
Accounts payable, accrual of............... 47
Accrual 39
Accrual basis of accounting............ 10, 58
Accrual concept.................................... 12
Accrued bonuses................................... 34
Accrued vacation pay 37
Accrued wages 33
Accumulated depreciation, calculation of
.... 28
Adjusting entries.................................. 40
Adjusting entry 14
Allowance for doubtful accounts.... 18, 42
Asset acquisition cost 23

Balance sheet... 5
Bank balance 44
Bank reconciliation, problems with...... 46
Billing and collections.......................... 16
Bonus, accrued 34
Budget versus actual review 50
Building asset account.......................... 22

Card reconciliation 19
Cash basis of accounting 10, 58
Chart of accounts................................... 1
Compound entry 14
Computer equipment asset account 22
Cost control 56
Cost of goods sold accounting 31
Credit.. 12, 58

Debit.. 11, 58
Depreciation 47
    Accumulated.................................... 28
    Concepts 24
    Journal entries................................. 27
    Method... 24
    Purpose of.. 23
Direct write-off method........................ 18
Disposal accounting.............................. 29
Disputed charges analysis.................... 20
Double entry accounting................. 11, 58

Employee advances................................36
Equipment asset account.......................22
Expense report form..............................20
Expense report processing.....................20
Expense report review...........................21

Financial analysis.................................51
Financial reporting best practices...........8
Financial statements, review of.............50
Fixed assets, disposal of.......................29
Fraud indicators 56
Furniture and fixtures asset account......22

Horizontal analysis................................50

Income statement 6
Income tax liability 50
Intangible asset definition 22

Journal entries 13
    Accrued expense 43
    Adjusting...40
    Reversing 40

Land definition......................................22
Land improvements definition 22
Leasehold improvement accounting......27
Leasehold improvements 22

MACRS depreciation.............................25
Manual paycheck entry 35
Matching principle 44
Mileage claim review............................21

Non-reimbursement expenses 21

Office equipment....................................23

Payroll journal entry.............................32
Payroll transactions..............................31
Per diem meal review............................21
Prepaid assets 43
Procurement cards.................................19
Purpose of financial statements..............8

Reserve updating 44
Revenue, accrual 39
Reversing entry.............................. 14, 40

Sales tax remittances 16
Salvage value....................................... 24
Software 23
Straight-line method 24

Tax deposit journal entry 39
Transaction recordation................... 11, 59

Useful life..24

Vacation pay, accrued 37
Vehicles 23

Wage accrual...................................33, 39

www.ingramcontent.com/pod-product-compliance
Lightning Source LLC
Chambersburg PA
CBHW051422200326
41520CB00023B/7329